WALKING ON GUERNSEY

About the Author

Paddy Dillon is a prolific walker and guidebook writer, with over 40 books to his name. He is an indefatigable long-distance walker who has walked all of Britain's National Trails and several major European trails. He has led guided walking holidays and has walked throughout Europe, as well as in Nepal, Tibet and the Rocky Mountains of Canada and the US.

Paddy has walked extensively around all the Channel Islands, delighting in island-hopping. While exploring Guernsey, Alderney, Sark and Herm he has walked around the coasts several times, enjoying urban promenades, sandy beach walks, cliff-top paths, rugged headlands and secluded coves. He has also penetrated far inland, along quiet traffic-calmed *ruettes tranquilles* and through intensively cultivated countryside.

Other Cicerone guides by the author:

WALKING ON GUERNSEY

by

Paddy Dillon

2 POLICE SQUARE, MILNTHORPE, CUMBRIA LA7 7PY
www.cicerone.co.uk

© Paddy Dillon 2011
First Edition 2011
ISBN: 978 1 85284 639 8

This book is one of two new guides to walking on the Channel Islands, replacing
Paddy Dillon's previous Cicerone guide:
Channel Island Walks
ISBN-10: 1 85284 288 1
ISBN-13: 978 1 85284 288 8

Printed by KHL Printing, Singapore.
A catalogue record for this book is available from the British Library.
All photographs are by the author.

Advice to Readers

Readers are advised that, while every effort is made by our authors to ensure
the accuracy of guidebooks as they go to print, changes can occur during
the lifetime of an edition. Please check Updates on this book's page on
the Cicerone website (www.cicerone.co.uk) before planning your trip. We
would also advise that you check information about such things as transport, accommodation and shops locally. Even rights of way can be altered
over time. We are always grateful for information about any discrepancies
between a guidebook and the facts on the ground, sent by email to info@
cicerone.co.uk or by post to Cicerone, 2 Police Square, Milnthorpe LA7
7PY, United Kingdom.

Front cover: Le Havre Gosselin, looking from Sark to Brecqhou

CONTENTS

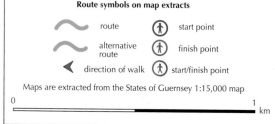

Route symbols on map extracts

route

start point

alternative route

finish point

direction of walk

start/finish point

Maps are extracted from the States of Guernsey 1:15,000 map

0   1 km

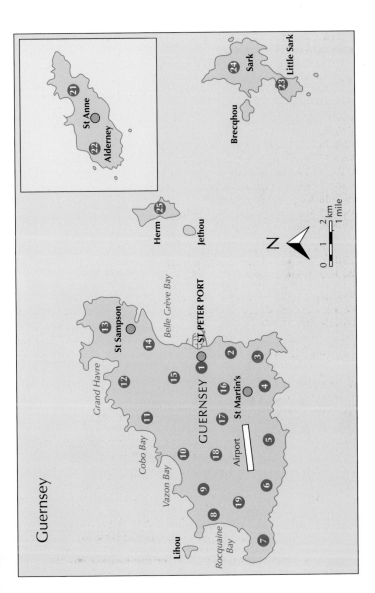

Guernsey

Attractively rugged rocks are seen while
walking round the Hommet headland (Walk 10)

INTRODUCTION

'Morceaux de France tombés à la mer
et ramassés par l'Angleterre.'
'Pieces of France fallen into the sea
and picked up by England.'

Victor Hugo

Small and often very busy, but also beautiful and abounding in interest, the Channel Islands are an intriguing walking destination. The self-governing 'bailiwicks' of Guernsey and Jersey owe their allegiance to the Crown and seem outwardly British, but are in fact an ancient remnant of the Duchy of Normandy, with Norman–French place-names very much in evidence. For British visitors, it is like being at home and abroad at the same time. French visitors, however, find it a quintessentially British experience!

Walkers will find magnificent cliff and coastal paths, golden sandy beaches, wooded valleys and quiet country lanes. Flowers will be noticed everywhere and there is a rich birdlife. There are castles, churches, ancient monuments and fortifications to visit, as well as a host of other attractions. There are efficient and frequent bus services, and easy onward links by air and sea between the islands. This guidebook describes 24 one-day walking routes, covering a total distance around 225km (140 miles), plus a long-distance coastal walk around the island of Guernsey, almost 65km (40 miles). There is also a note about the Channel Islands Way, a long-distance island-hopping route embracing the entire archipelago, covering 178km (110 miles).

LOCATION

The Channel Islands lie south of Britain, but not everyone immediately appreciates how close they are to France. The islands fit snugly into a box bounded by lines of longitude 2°W and 3°W, and lines of latitude 49°N and 50°N. This puts them well and truly in the Golfe de St Malo off the Normandy coast of France, The French refer to them as *Les Îles Anglo-Normandes*, and that is the clue to their curious place in geography and history. They are the only remnants of the Duchy of Normandy to remain loyal to the Crown.

Guernsey is the second largest of the Channel Islands after Jersey, with an area of only 63km² (24½ square miles). The smaller neighbouring islands of Alderney, Sark and Herm together add less than 15km² (6 square miles) of land area. No point on Guernsey is more than 3km (2 miles) from the sea, yet it can take weeks to explore the place thoroughly.

GEOLOGY

In Britain virtually every major geological period is represented. Channel Islands geology is more closely related to structures in France. Rocks are either very ancient or relatively recent, with hundreds of millions of years missing from the middle of the geological timescale. Fossils are virtually absent and the amount of sedimentary rock is quite limited. Most of the area is made up of ancient sediments and igneous rocks which have been heated,

warped, crushed, deformed, melted and metamorphosed. Further intrusions of igneous rocks cause further confusion for the beginner, but there is a basic succession that can be presented in a simplified form.

The most ancient bedrocks in the Channel Islands are metamorphic and metasedimentary rocks known as 'Pentevrian' – a term used in neighbouring France. Ancient gneisses, often containing xenoliths of other long-lost strata, feature in this early series. Dating rocks of this type is possible only by examining radio-isotopes in their mineral structure, which suggest dates of formation ranging from 2500 to 1000 million years ago. The oldest rocks occur in southern Guernsey, western Alderney and possibly on Sark.

Rugged cliff scenery is enjoyed from the path all the way round Icart Point (Walk 4)

The 'Brioverian' sedimentary series dates from 900 to 700 million years ago. This is represented by a broad band of mudstones, siltstones and conglomerates across Jersey. In Guernsey, however, only a small area in the west contains these rocks, though in an altered state. One of the problems of dealing with these sediments is that even while they were being formed, they were being deformed by earthquakes, heat and pressure. Fossil remains are few, and in fact are represented only by a few worm burrows.

Following on from the formation of the Brioverian sediments, a series of igneous intrusions were squeezed into the bedrock around 650 to 500 million years ago. Interestingly, both granites and gabbros were intruded, along with intermediate rock types. A host of minor sills, dykes and pipes were injected to further complicate matters. These tough, speckled, igneous rocks have been quarried all over the Channel Islands for local building and export.

Events during the next 500 million years are conjectural, and based on geological happenings elsewhere in Britain and France. Rocks from this span of time are absent, though they are known from the surrounding sea bed. On dry land, sediments date only from the past couple of million years, and as this was a time of ice ages, indications are that the climate varied from sub-tropical to sub-arctic. Sea levels fluctuated so that both raised beaches and sunken forests and peat bogs can be discerned. For much of the time, the Channel Islands were part of one land mass with Britain and France, but rising sea levels formed the English Channel and, one by one, each of the Channel Islands. Guernsey became an island around 14,000 years ago, while Jersey became an island around 7000 years ago.

Exhibits relating to the geology of Guernsey can be studied at the Guernsey Museum. The British Geological Survey publishes detailed geological maps of the Channel Islands and there are a number of publications dealing with the subject.

TURBULENT HISTORY

Little is known of the customs and traditions of nomadic Palaeolithic Man, but he hunted mammoth and woolly rhinoceros when Guernsey was still part of the European mainland 200,000 years ago. Neolithic and Bronze Age people made many magnificent monuments which are dotted around the Channel Islands. Henges, mounds, tombs and mysterious menhirs were raised by peoples whose origins are unclear and whose language is unknown. What is certain is that they had a reverence for their dead and were obviously living in well-ordered communities able to turn their hands to the construction of such mighty structures. The Romans knew of these islands, though whether they wholly colonised them or simply

Ancient burial chambers, such as Le Déhus Dolmen, are sometimes big enough to stand up inside (Walk 13)

had an occupying presence and trading links is a matter of debate.

St Sampson brought the Christian message to Guernsey in the 6th century. The basic parish structure of the Channel Islands, and most of the parish churches, date from around this period. No doubt the position of the Channel Islands made it a favourite spot for plundering by all and sundry on the open sea. The Norsemen were regular raiders in the 9th century, and by the 10th century the islands were well established in the territory of Normandy. It was from Normandy that Duke William I, 'The Longsword', claimed the islands as his own in the year 933, and they have been part of the Duchy of Normandy ever since.

Duke William II, 'The Conqueror', defeated Harold at the Battle of Hastings in 1066. When King John lost Normandy to France in 1204, the Channel Islands remained loyal and were granted special privileges and a measure of self-government that continues to this day. However, the islands were repeatedly attacked, invaded and partially occupied by French forces throughout the Hundred Years War. During the most turbulent times of strife, the Pope himself intervened and decreed in 1483 that the Channel Islands should be neutral in those conflicts. The islanders were able to turn the situation to their advantage, trading with both sides! Church control passed from the French Diocese of Coutances to the English Diocese of Winchester in 1568.

During the English Civil War in the 17th century, the islands were divided against themselves, with Guernsey for Parliament and Jersey for the Crown. The French invaded the islands for the last time in 1781; stout defensive structures were raised against any further threats, particularly during the Napoleonic Wars, and in fact well into the 19th century. Queen Victoria visited the Channel Islands three times to inspect military developments.

During the First World War the Channel Islands escaped virtually unscathed, though the local militia forces were disbanded, and many of those who joined the regular army were slaughtered elsewhere in Europe. In the Second World War, after the fall of France to the German army, the Channel Islands were declared indefensible and were demilitarised. Many islanders evacuated to England, particularly from Alderney, but others stayed behind and suffered for five years under the German Occupation. Massive fortifications made the Channel Islands the most heavily defended part of Hitler's Atlantic Wall.

There were only token raids and reconnaissances by British forces, and the Channel Islands were completely by-passed during the D-Day landings in nearby Normandy. VE Day in Europe was 8th May 1945, but the Channel Islands were not liberated until 9th May, as it was unclear whether the German garrison would surrender without a fight. The Channel Islands Occupation Society, www.occupied.guernsey.net, publishes a number of books and journals about

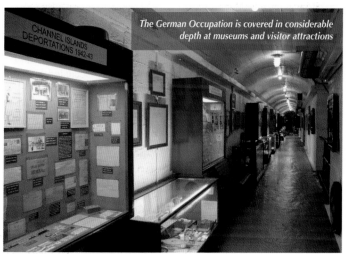

The German Occupation is covered in considerable depth at museums and visitor attractions

the war years, including an annual review. Various military structures from the Occupation have been preserved as visitor attractions.

The modern development of the Channel Islands has been in two directions. As a holiday destination it caters for a multitude of tastes, with an emphasis on sun, sea, fun, family, good food and the outdoors. In the financial services sector the low rate of taxation has brought in billions of pounds of investment and attracted a population of millionaires. The Channel Islands retain some quirky laws and customs, enjoy a low crime rate, issue their own currency and postage stamps and enjoy a unique history and heritage that is well interpreted at a number of interesting visitor sites.

The best place to start enquiring into history is the Guernsey Museum, Candie Gardens, St Peter Port, GY1 1UG, tel. 01481 726518. This is also the place to enquire about La Société Guernesiaise, tel. 01481 725093, www.societe.org.gg, and the Guernsey Museums and Galleries service, www.museum.guernsey.net. A 'Heritage Pass' can be purchased, allowing entry to all the sites managed by the service. There are numerous publications available examining all aspects of Channel Islands history. Detail is often intense, and any historical building or site mentioned in this guidebook probably has one or more books dedicated entirely to it.

Another organisation involved with heritage matters is the National Trust of Guernsey, 26 Cornet Street, St Peter Port, GY1 1LF, tel. 01481 728451, www.nationaltrust-gsy.org. gg. The Trust owns land and properties around Guernsey, several of which are visited on walks throughout this guide. Some properties are leased to tenants and cannot be visited, while others may have limited opening times. The National Trust of Guernsey has reciprocal agreements with the National Trust for Jersey, National Trust of England, Wales and Northern Ireland, and National Trust for Scotland, allowing members free entry to properties that normally levy a charge.

GOVERNMENT

The Channel Islands form a quirky little archipelago, with startling divisions among themselves. They are neither colonies nor dependencies; they are not part of the United Kingdom or the European Union. They have been described as 'Peculiars of the Crown', meaning that they are practically the property of the Crown, and they owe their allegiance to the Crown, but not to Parliament.

There are actually two self-governing 'bailiwicks' whose law-making processes are quite separate from those of the United Kingdom's Parliament. Furthermore, the Bailiwick of Guernsey's affairs are quite separate from the Bailiwick of Jersey. A thorough investigation of Channel Islands government is an absorbing study, which anyone with

Guernsey is not part of the United Kingdom, but owes its allegiance to the British Crown

political inclinations might like to investigate while walking around the islands. The Bailiwick of Guernsey embraces Alderney and Sark, but those islands have their own governments. For further information check the States of Guernsey government website, www.gov.gg, the States of Alderney government website, www.alderney.gov.gg and the Chief Pleas of Sark website, www.gov.sark.gg. Sark was the last feudal state in Europe, but embraced democracy by holding its first general elections at the end of 2008 and 2010.

WILDLIFE

Plants

The Channel Islands are noted for their flowers, and it is possible to find wild flowers in bloom at any time of the year. The southerly, maritime disposition of the islands and their range of habitats, from fertile soil to barren rocks, ensure that a wide variety of species can thrive. Even attempting to shortlist them is a pointless exercise, with hundreds of species growing around the islands. Bear in mind that the sea is also a bountiful source of plants, with the tiny Lihou Island surrounded by 130 species of seaweed. Add to this the plants that are cultivated in greenhouses and gardens and the study of Guernsey's floral tributes becomes a vast undertaking!

Even walkers who have no great interest in flora cannot fail to be amazed at the sight of rampant flowers growing around the rugged coast and hedgerows of Guernsey. Add abundant swathes of sea campion and red campion, blazes of gorse and broom and nodding ox-eye daisies,

15

Fleshy-leaved mesembryanthemum is common and was once used to camouflage concrete bunkers

and the result is a riot of colour. The sight of fleshy-leaved mesembryanthemum colonising entire cliffs is impressive and unusual. A comprehensive field guide to wild flowers is an essential companion on any walk, but make sure that it encompasses not only a good range of British plants but also plants from the Mediterranean, which are at their northernmost limits around Guernsey. La Société Guernesiaise, www.societe.org.gg, gathers plenty of information about Guernsey's botany.

Animals

Mammoth, woolly rhinoceros and deer are known to have flourished on the Channel Islands, but today the islands are devoid of large wild mammals. Rabbits do well almost

everywhere, but little else is likely to be seen except for evidence of moles and small rodents. Look to the sea for other species, such as dolphins. Local differences occur between the islands, such as the fact that toads are found on Jersey, but not Guernsey, though green lizards live on both islands. Insect life is abundant and varied, with a range of colourful butterflies.

The birdlife is amazingly rich, with a range of residents and a host of migratory species. While the landmass is rather small to support many raptors, there are owls, kestrels and sparrowhawks. The coastal margins abound in interest, attracting a range of waders that probe the beaches and rock pools for food. The cliffs and pebbly beaches provide safe nesting

16

places for a variety of gulls and terns. At the right time of year puffins can be seen on some of the smaller islands and stacks, while a large population of gannets can be seen near Alderney. There are small areas of heathland where the rare Dartford warbler may be seen or heard, and there are a few areas of dense woodland, marsh and grassland which attract particular species. The range of bird habitats is under pressure from human development and recreation on such tiny islands but, even so, there is plenty to see.

Listing a couple of hundred species of birds is a pointless exercise, and so much depends on the time of year and prevailing conditions. A good field guide to birds is useful, and there are titles which are specific to the Channel Islands. The Guernsey Museum has exhibits relating to the natural history of the island. La Société Guernesiaise, www.societe.org.gg, collects information for the annual Guernsey Bird Report, or see www.guernseybirds.org.gg for information. Similar organisations include the Alderney Society, www.alderneysociety.org, and La Société Sercquaise, www.socsercq.sark.gg.

The National Trust of Guernsey is a major landowner, maintaining some interesting short walks

PROTECTED AREAS

There is no national park on Guernsey, but there are several small nature reserves, ranging from marshland to woodland. The National Trust of Guernsey has already been mentioned, which is dedicated to preserving areas of land around the island. There are also large and very important marine reserves, some of which are particularly difficult to access. These include an area around Lihou and an area stretching west of Alderney.

The little yellow aeroplane called 'Joey' is easily the most well-known aircraft in the Channel Islands

GETTING TO GUERNSEY

A map of transport routes makes Guernsey look like the centre of the universe, with ferries and flights converging on the island from all points of the compass. Bear in mind that there are seasonal variations, with more services available in the summer months than in the winter.

WHO CAN GO?

People who hold British or European Union passports or identity cards do not need visas to visit Guernsey. All air travellers must produce some form of photo-ID or they may be denied boarding. People who have obtained a visa to visit Britain can also visit Guernsey during the period

for which their visa is valid. Dogs and other pets can be brought from Britain to Guernsey, subject to any conditions that might be imposed by ferry or flight operators. Usual practice applies to walking dogs in the countryside. Keep them under control, especially near livestock. Dogs may be barred from beaches during the summer months and anti-fouling laws are in place everywhere.

FLIGHTS

Direct flights to Guernsey operate from around a dozen British airports, along with a few direct flights from countries such as Ireland, France and Germany. Both scheduled and charter flights are available. Scheduled flights are mostly operated by Aurigny, www. aurigny.com and Flybe, www.flybe. com. Aurigny and Blue Islands, www. blueislands.com, operate inter-island flights. Summer charter flights are mainly operated by Channel Islands Travel Group, www.guernseytravel. com. This is not an exhaustive list and choices are quite bewildering, so it takes time to sift and sort between the operators, schedules and prices, but with patience some extraordinarily good deals can be found.

Ferries serve Guernsey from Britain and France. Ferries from Britain are operated by Condor, www.condor ferries.co.uk, sailing from Weymouth, Poole and Portsmouth. Passengers can choose between fast and slow ships, with links to and from Jersey. Condor also serves Guernsey from St Malo in France. Other ferry services from France are operated by Manche Îles Express, www.manche-iles-express.com, sailing from Diélette, also offering links with Jersey and Alderney, as well as sailing between Jersey and Sark.

Package holidays to the Channel Islands can be arranged for any period from a weekend upwards, freeing you from the hassle of trying to co-ordinate ferries, flights, accommodation and meals. Prices are quite competitive and there are seasonal variations, so it pays to shop around for the best deals.

Castle Cornet has witnessed centuries of change at St Peter Port

WHEN TO GO

Guernsey is suitable as a year-round destination and generally enjoys slightly milder weather than the south of England, but the weather is still highly variable and impossible to forecast accurately. Winters are mild, but there may be frosts and, very occasionally, snow. Very bad weather at any time of year can upset ferry schedules, while fog affects flights. The peak summer period can be very hot and busy, which may not suit those looking for peace and quiet. The shoulder seasons, spring and autumn, are generally ideal for walking, with bright, clear days and temperatures that are neither too high nor too low. In fact, these are the times of year that the Guernsey Walking Weeks are arranged, featuring plenty of guided walks led by local experts.

ACCOMMODATION

Guernsey offers every type of accommodation to suit every pocket, but over the past few years prices have risen as hotels have moved up-market. Choose an accommodation base carefully, thinking primarily about how you intend to organise your walks. If you are hiring a car, then any base anywhere on the island will be fine. If you intend using the bus services to travel to and from walks, then the best base would be somewhere central in St Peter Port, handy for the bus station. An annual

Walking and cycling are popular, especially on the coast where there may be shared use paths

accommodation guide is produced, which can be obtained by post from Visit Guernsey, or browsed online at www.visitguernsey.com.

There are no nasty diseases on Guernsey or, at least, nothing you couldn't contract at home. Domestic water supplies are fed from either reservoirs or underground sources, but there has been no desalination plant in operation for decades. Treated water is perfectly drinkable, but some people don't like the taste and prefer to buy bottled water, which is quite expensive. There are no snakes and no stinging insects worse than wasps and honey-bees.

In case of a medical emergency, dial 999 (or the European emergency number 112) for an ambulance. In case of a non-emergency there are chemists, doctors, dentists and a hospital. At the time of writing (and this may change) there is no reciprocal health agreement between Guernsey and the United Kingdom, nor is there any point in carrying the European Health Insurance Card. If emergency treatment is required it will be provided, but in order to avoid charges it is necessary to carry appropriate insurance.

FOOD AND DRINK

Guernsey has long prided itself on being intensively agricultural, though this is waning and farmers face an uncertain future. In the past, people would think of 'Guernsey tomatoes', when the island was famous for its tomato greenhouses, but production has become uneconomic and many greenhouses now lie derelict or have been demolished. Some greenhouses are now purely involved in the production of flowers. At one time, Guernsey was the world's leading producer of marmalade!

The name 'Guernsey' also conjures images of contented brown-and-white cows giving rich, creamy milk for butter and ice-cream. Guernsey cows have a long pedigree, having apparently lived on the island for over 1000 years and have always been immensely important. Guernsey herds are admired and renowned and have been exported world-wide. They even have their own website, www.guernseycattle.com.

Naturally, Guernsey offers good seafood, but one of the greatest delicacies is unlikely to be savoured by visitors. The 'ormer', or abalone, is a marine mollusc that can only be gathered at certain times and there are plenty of restrictions in place to conserve the species. As a result it tends to be eaten primarily by Guernsey folk, with nothing left over for commercial restaurants.

One of the most notable staple Guernsey foodstuffs is a moist fruit loaf known as 'Guernsey Gâche', whose flavour allows it to be eaten with a range of sweet and savoury food. Of course, it goes very well spread with rich Guernsey butter and eaten with a slice of Guernsey cheese. When fresh fruit and vegetables are required, visitors are often surprised to find these for sale from unmanned stalls beside roads all over the island. The idea is to help yourself to home-grown produce and leave payment in an honesty box, though judging by some of the notices attached to the stalls, some people simply steal from them, raising a question mark over how long this mode of selling can endure.

Of course, Guernsey also imports plenty of food and drink, both British and international goods, from simple, low-priced products to expensive quality items. On the whole, expect things to cost a little more than in Britain, and bear in mind that most supermarkets and shops are in St Peter Port, and not every village has a shop. On the other hand, pubs, restaurants, cafés and snack kiosks are regularly encountered while walking round Guernsey, and places offering refreshments are mentioned in the route descriptions. Food offered ranges from basic snacks to haute cuisine, and as it is easy to get from place to place for food and drink, you need only be guided by your palate and spending limits.

PARLEZ-VOUS FRANGLAIS?

For centuries the language commonly spoken around the Channel Islands was a Norman–French 'patois' which had distinct forms from island to

Guernsey cows feed on lush grass and give rich and creamy milk for butter and ice cream

island. The Guernsey form is known as *Guernésiaise*, or even *Dgèrnésiais* and, while it is rarely heard, it is still spoken and some people are keen to preserve it. Sometimes it is referred to as 'Guernsey French', but a French person would struggle to understand it. It also goes by the name of 'Guernsey Norman French'. The Alderney form of *Aurignaise* has perished and the Sark form of *Sercquaise* is spoken only by a handful of people.

Visiting walkers may hear nothing of the language, but will be very aware of the roots of the language preserved in place-names all over the islands. Motorists on Guernsey struggling to find a place to park will often be confronted by signs warning *'ces premises sont terre à l'amende'*, followed by a threat of a fine levied by the Royal Court. If you are lucky, the notice may also state 'no parking' in English.

Visitors with a good knowledge of French will probably pronounce the place-names with a French accent, but in fact the 'correct' pronunciation would be different. In all other respects, English is spoken, written and understood everywhere, but there are also sizeable resident, working and visiting nationals from many other countries. It is increasingly common to hear several languages spoken on the streets. If assistance is needed with the pronunciation of a place-name, the best person to ask is a Guernsey person!

MONEY

The States of Guernsey issue their own banknotes and coins, which are inextricably linked to Sterling and come in exactly the same denominations. However, Guernsey £1 and £2 coins are rare, while Guernsey £1 notes are common. Bank of England Sterling notes and coins can be spent in Guernsey, and currency issued by the States of Jersey is also accepted. In theory Sterling banknotes from Scotland and Northern Ireland are accepted, but this depends on whether the person to whom they are being offered is familiar with them. Some businesses will accept Euros, but the rate of exchange may be poor.

Change given at the close of a transaction may be a mixture of Guernsey and British currency. Remember that Guernsey currency is not legal tender in Britain, though British banks will change notes at face value. It is common for visitors approaching the end of a holiday in Guernsey to request British currency only in their change. Your last few Guernsey coins can be dropped in a charity box on departure, or saved as mementos of your visit.

Guernsey specialises in financial services, and banks from all over the world are represented on the streets of St Peter Port. ATMs are common and a wide variety of credit and debit cards are accepted by businesses. There is no VAT added to purchases and the island enjoys a low rate of tax. There is an advantage in purchasing some high-value items on the island, but the cost of transporting goods to Guernsey can make some of the benefits marginal.

COMMUNICATIONS

If taking a mobile phone to Guernsey, check in advance with your service provider, or you might find yourself paying a high price for calls. The local provider is Sure Cable & Wireless,

www.surecw.com. There is generally good mobile coverage around the island. There are telephone kiosks in most urban and some rural areas, which take coins and cards, and emergency calls (999 or 112) are free. Free Wi-Fi is available at the tourist information centre in St Peter Port and some accommodation providers also offer this as a service to their guests.

Royal Mail postage stamps from Britain are not valid in Guernsey. Any attempt to use them will result in delayed delivery and an excess charge for the recipient. Guernsey Post stamps must be used, and if you are posting to Britain, Europe or any other destination, make this clear when you buy stamps as there are different rates. There are 10 post offices around Guernsey, and one each on Alderney, Sark and Herm. Walkers with an interest in philately can make arrangements to collect Guernsey stamps and first-day covers on a regular basis, see www. guernseypost.com.

Telephone and postal services on Guernsey are different from those operating in the United Kingdom

Looking along the southernmost coast of Guernsey to Pointe de la Moye (Walk 5)

WALKING ON GUERNSEY

Almost a tropical scene, as walkers take a break at a well-appointed beach café

The walks in this guidebook are mostly short and straightforward, chosen to reflect the diversity of the landscapes and seascapes, along with the history, heritage and natural history of Guernsey. Almost all the walks link directly with one or two other walks, allowing all kinds of extensions to the routes. All the walks are easily accessible by bus services, so a car is not necessary.

The islands covered by the Bailiwick of Guernsey have a combined land area of 78km² (30 square miles) and walkers are never more than 3km (2 miles) from the sea. Within this limited area this guidebook offers around 225km (140 miles) of incredibly varied walking, with a coastal walk alone measuring almost 65km (40 miles). If explorations are extended beyond Guernsey, Alderney, Sark and Herm to Jersey, then the interest and enjoyment is doubled. Complete coastal walks around the five main Channel Islands are now being promoted as the 'Channel Islands Way', measuring 178km (110 miles).

In the past the Channel Islands were not really viewed as a walking destination. Rather, they were a holiday destination where people simply couldn't help walking. These days, one third of visitors state that their main reason for visiting the islands is to walk. The sight of golden beaches, rugged cliffs, flowery headlands and lush woodlands prove irresistible for exploring on foot. There are so many things to see along the paths, tracks and roads – interesting places to visit and always the offer of food and drink.

The walks are mostly circular and almost every stretch along the coast features a contrasting exploration inland. It has to be said that there are few paths and tracks inland, and while some roads can be quite busy, there are plenty of quiet country roads too, specially designated as *ruettes tranquilles*, where priority is given to walkers, cyclists and horse-riders. A few of the walks are entirely inland, because it is important to appreciate the inland countryside and its farming traditions just as much as the popular coastline. Almost every route passes some sort of attraction, ranging from castles to historic houses, churches to craft centres. Many attractions seem to exist purely because they have a captive audience of visitors; those that are on or near the walks are noted, with brief details offered. Many of them have an entry charge and may be well worth an hour's exploration.

Paths on Guernsey are mostly on firm, dry surfaces, but some stretches may be muddy after rain. Some paths on steep slopes are equipped with plenty of concrete steps. Most of the time a pair of comfortable walking shoes are fine for walking, and hefty boots are not required. If boots are worn, lightweight ones will suffice.

There are plenty of walking opportunities inland on Guernsey, where there is a network of lanes

There are some signposts, but most paths are obvious even without markers, and it is usually obvious if a path is private. Roads on Guernsey sometimes bear their names at one end or both, which saves confusion when they form a dense network.

WHAT TO TAKE

Generally speaking, Guernsey's weather is a little milder than the weather you would expect in the south of England. There are no hills and walkers rarely find themselves much above 100m (330ft) above sea level. The most basic walking gear will suffice, with comfortable footwear, clothing to suit hot and cool conditions, including sun protection for sunny days and waterproofs in

case of rain. It is increasingly common to see heavily-booted walkers with poles and packs trudging round the island, but Guernsey is a gentle landscape, and even if foul weather were to interfere with a walk, it is very easy to cut walks short, bail out by bus and retreat to your lodgings.

WAYMARKING AND ACCESS

Guernsey is intensively cultivated, with large areas given over to tillage and greenhouses, while most pastures are grazed by Guernsey cows. Around 60,000 people live on the island, the road network is remarkably dense and car ownership is very high. Add to this the huge number of visitors, and it is a wonder there is room to breathe, let alone walk. However, there are plenty

Prominent stone markers often indicate where paths are leading, especially around the coast

of paths, tracks and quiet roads available for walkers, and while signposts and waymarks are few, routes freely available to the public are usually quite obvious. The best maps of Guernsey show many of these routes, but by no means all of them. By contrast, paths, tracks and roads that are private are usually clearly marked as such. In practical terms, with this guidebook to hand, Guernsey can be explored thoroughly using the available access.

Special mention needs to be made of the inter-tidal zone. Guernsey has one of the biggest tidal ranges in the world, up to 12m (40ft) at spring tides. The sight of sandy beaches and jagged rocks emerging from the sea as the tide recedes encourages many people to explore to the water's edge, and to a certain extent this is to be encouraged, but it must be done with caution. Obtain a copy of the tide times and study them carefully. Walking out as the tide recedes is unlikely to be a problem, but when the tide is advancing it is possible to be cut off before realising it. Trying to get from beach to beach around the foot of cliffs can be dangerous and can lead to an inconvenient stranding, or death by drowning. In short, do not wander around the inter-tidal zone without having a clearly visible route back to dry land.

MAPS

The maps in this guidebook are extracted from the 1:15,000 States of Guernsey map. This is rather different from the Ordnance Survey maps used by most walkers in Britain. In fact, the map was originally compiled by the Military Survey at 1:25,000, but this is now out of print. New and updated digital mapping has been produced by Digimap at 1:15,000, www.digimap. gg, for the States of Guernsey. This is the most detailed map of the island, showing everything down to field boundaries and even the back gardens of houses in towns and villages. The walking routes in this guidebook are shown as a highlighted overlay on this 1:15,000 map. Sketch maps of Alderney, Sark and Herm show the walking routes on the small islands.

There are plenty of other maps of Guernsey, mostly published by Perry's. These include free maps suitable for general touring, which often highlight attractions so boldly that they obscure other details in the vicinity. By all means amass a collection of free maps, picking them up from the tourist information centre or from hotels and visitor attractions around the island.

GETTING AROUND GUERNSEY

By car

Cars can be taken on the Condor ferries to Guernsey, and it is possible to hire cars on Guernsey, either pre-booked or on arrival. Guernsey cars carry only numbers on their registration plates, but hire cars are stamped with a prominent 'H' for 'hire', or according to local drivers, 'horror', because of the way they perceive the

A designated ruette tranquille gives priority to walkers and cyclists and has a 15mph speed limit.

driving skills of visitors! Guernsey's roads are narrow and the maximum speed limit is 35mph, dropping to 15mph on *ruettes tranquilles*. Roads can be very congested, especially at peak times around St Peter Port, and parking is very limited in some areas. The bottom line is, you won't be going anywhere fast!

A car is essential if you choose accommodation away from a regular bus route, but if you are based in St Peter Port, or on a regular bus route, then it is best to use buses to travel round the island. Drivers who do not understand the 'filter in turn' rule that applies in Guernsey should think twice before driving there.

By bus

Guernsey has an excellent bus network provided by Island Coachways,

30

possibly one of the best networks in the entire world! It is worth visiting the bus station to pick up timetables and enquire about the 'Ormer Card' at the earliest opportunity. All the routes in this guidebook were researched using buses, and the author heartily recommends this mode of travel.

The bus timetable is most comprehensive and it needs to be studied carefully. Bus routes are numbered, and some routes run clockwise and anti-clockwise, or have north and south variants. The most popular routes, 7 and 7A, run clockwise and anti-clockwise around the coast of Guernsey, while other routes are shorter and generally describe loops inland, occasionally touching the coast. Many bus routes run along the same roads, or cross over each other, and of course all of them run from, and back to, St Peter Port.

Tickets can be bought on the buses and there is a flat fare, payable no matter whether you are going one stop, or all the way round the island. Although the fare is cheap, it is still worth obtaining an 'Ormer Card', which is Guernsey's tongue-in-cheek version of London's 'Oyster Card'. The card needs to be pre-charged with journeys, paid for in advance. The more journeys you add, the cheaper each journey becomes, until each journey becomes 50% of the cost of buying a ticket on the bus. On boarding each bus, simply place the card on a machine, which will issue a ticket stating how many journeys remain on the card. One card can serve any number of people – simply keep placing it on the machine to obtain a ticket for each person travelling. It might seem complicated at first, but it really is a simple system. The hardest part lies in trying to figure out how many bus journeys you are likely to make during your time on Guernsey. During the summer months there are slightly extended services, but on the whole there is little difference between summer and winter. Buses run from early until late, all over the island. For full details of all bus services on Guernsey, tel. 01481 720210, www.icw.gg/buses.

The small islands of Alderney, Sark and Herm are usually reached from Guernsey. There are no ferries from Guernsey to Alderney, but Manche Îles Express, www.manche-iles-express.com, serves Alderney from Diélette in France, and serves Sark from Jersey. Flights between Guernsey and Alderney are operated by Aurigny, www.aurigny.com and Blue Islands, www.blueislands.com. Ferries from Guernsey to Sark are provided by the Isle of Sark Shipping Company, www.sarkshippingcompany.com. Ferries from Guernsey to Herm are provided by Travel Trident, tel. 01481 721379.

Alderney, Sark and Herm do not have bus services. There are tour

Guernsey probably has one of the best bus networks in the world, and proves remarkably good value

buses and taxis on Alderney, while Sark has a limited tractor and trailer service, along with horse-drawn carriages. On Herm visitors are expected to walk everywhere, but the island is tiny and all who visit the place expect to walk.

TOURIST INFORMATION

The first point of contact for all tourism-related enquiries is Guernsey Information Centre, North Plantation, St Peter Port, GY1 2LQ, tel. 01481 723552, email enquiries@visitguernsey. com, website www.visitguernsey.com.

The information centre can provide plenty of free printed materials, including accommodation brochures and leaflets about attractions, events and 'what's on' guides. There are also books, maps and gifts on sale. The website includes plenty of information about walking opportunities, including the popular Guernsey Walking Weeks that are a feature of spring and autumn each year. These events offer visiting walkers the chance to explore the island in the company of Guernsey people, led by knowledgeable local guides, www.healthspan. co.uk/walkingweek.

There are also tourism bodies on the smaller islands. For Alderney, check with Visit Alderney, States of Alderney, PO Box 1, Alderney, GY9 3AA, tel. 01481 822811, www. visitalderney.com. For Sark, check www.sark.info. For Herm, check www.herm.com.

EMERGENCIES

The police, ambulance, fire and coastguard services are all alerted by dialling 999, free of charge, from any telephone. Alternatively, the European emergency number of 112 can be used.

The emergency services sometimes call on the assistance of the Channel Islands Air Search, a voluntary organisation that maintains a light aircraft, available on stand-by 24 hours a day, 365 days a year, offering an 'eyes in the sky' capability around the islands. See www.ci-airsearch. com.

USING THIS GUIDE

The walks in this guidebook start with a town trail around St Peter Port, allowing visitors to become acquainted with some of the heritage features and services of the second largest town in the Channel Islands. Walks 2 to 14 are arranged clockwise round the coast of Guernsey, and most of them are circular, made up of a coastal stretch and an inland stretch. They are all fairly short and easy, with the most rugged being along the south coast. As all the walks are arranged side-by-side they can be linked to form longer walks. Walk 8 includes an optional extension that is entirely dependent on a favourable tide; therefore, it might not be possible to attempt while you are on the island. Walks 15 to 19 explore the inland parts of Guernsey, though as has already been observed, no

Quiet reflection – an early morning scene on the harbour at St Peter Port

part of the island is more than 3km (2 miles) from the sea.

Some walkers visit Guernsey simply to walk all the way round the coast, and this is an admirable plan. Walk 20 explains in very brief detail how to do it, by referring readers back to Walks 2 to 14. Each of these walks includes a stretch of coast, but at the point where these routes head inland, it is possible to link directly with the next walk in the book and the next stretch of coast. An annual sponsored walk aims to cover the coast in one long day, while average walkers would take three days to walk round the island.

All the walking routes on Guernsey are accessible by bus services, and if any other bus services cross them, these are mentioned.

Places offering food and drink are mentioned, but as opening times vary, it is wise to carry something to eat and drink. If there are any visitor attractions on the routes a brief description is given; if contact details are provided, opening times can be checked. Bear in mind that some attractions take an hour or two to explore properly, and this eats into the time spent walking. A very short walking route with two or three major attractions and a good restaurant can take all day to complete if walkers really want to make the most of these opportunities!

Walks 21 to 25 explore the small islands of Alderney, Sark and Herm, and so require onward travel from Guernsey to complete. These can be attempted as out-and-back day trips, using the earliest and latest transport

33

Channel Islands Way walkers can follow rugged cliff-top paths round the island of Jersey

links. It is better to spend a couple of days on both Alderney and Sark, so that the walking is not rushed, and the routes on those islands are presented with that in mind.

Walkers who have also obtained a copy of the Cicerone guidebook

Walking on Jersey can combine coastal walks around Guernsey, Alderney, Sark and Herm with a coastal walk around Jersey, thereby completing the 'Channel Islands Way'. The full distance is around 178km (110 miles).

WALK 1

St Peter Port Town Trail

Distance	Variable
Terrain	Urban roads, sometimes steep or with steps, as well as parks.
Start/Finish	Liberation Monument, St Peter Port
Refreshments	Plenty of choice around St Peter Port.
Transport	All bus services on Guernsey operate to and from the bus station on South Esplanade.

St Peter Port is the largest town on Guernsey and the second largest in the Channel Islands. Approaching the town by ferry, its buildings look as if they are stacked onto a cliff face, and the land certainly rises very abruptly from the harbour. A rigid route description is hardly appropriate, and in fact there is no need to dedicate a whole day to a tour. Simply explore a different area of town any time you are passing through. There are so many places of interest, many of them apparent even if you are not particularly on the lookout for them. Lots of little plaques and memorials are fixed to all sorts of structures. There is a fine museum, several interesting and historic buildings, steep and narrow streets, some with flights of steps, and a number of green spaces to discover. Free town plans are widely available.

The focal point for exploring **St Peter Port** is around the Weighbridge and the Liberation Monument between the harbour and a large marina. Truck-loads of tomatoes and other goods for shipment used to be weighed and then weighed again unladen at the Weighbridge. The difference between the two weights was the weight of the goods, for which payment would be made. Wandering along the North Esplanade leads past the **Guernsey Information Centre**, tel. 01481 723552, and onto The Quay. The bus station lies beyond on South Esplanade. ▶ High Street runs parallel to The Quay, in effect doubling back a few steps inland from the **Parish Church** of St Peter Port. The church is worth a visit; it dates from at least 1048, when it was referred to as Sancti Petri de Portu Maris.

Walk 2 starts on South Esplanade.

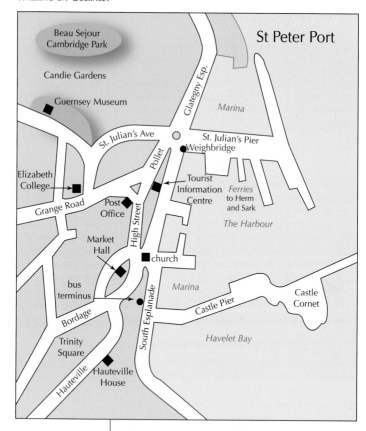

St Peter Port

The old **Market Hall** is tucked away behind the church, but has been converted into shops and no longer features market stalls. There are plenty of shops along High Street, continuing along The Pollet, offering goods at duty-free prices. At the post office on Smith Street enquiries can be made about Guernsey and Alderney stamps and first day covers. Climbing through St Peter Port is a matter of following steep and narrow streets, or very steep and very narrow streets, or even flights of

Buildings rise straight from the harbourside in St Peter Port and narrow streets climb inland

steps. Energetic walkers might dash up and down these, but most people will take them slowly and easily.

St Julian's Avenue rises fairly gently from the Liberation Monument and can be used to reach the **Candie Gardens**. A statue of Victor Hugo stands here and there are views across the harbour to the islands of Herm, Jethou and Sark. Sitting in the heart of the gardens is the **Guernsey Museum**, tel. 01481 726518, and there is an entry charge. This is a good starting point for those wishing to enquire into the history, natural history and heritage of the island. Despite limited space it tells the story of Guernsey from its bedrock upwards.

Visitors are often intrigued to see stone towers on the skyline when approaching St Peter Port by sea. These include Victoria Tower, Elizabeth College, St James' Centre and church spires. Walking from one to another involves negotiating a network of narrow streets, and if a route can be contrived down to the lovely green space of **Trinity Square**, then explorations can continue with some sense of order. Along the way some of the financial institutions that take advantage of Guernsey's low taxation rate can be seen.

A flight of steps near Trinity Square, alongside the Victoria Homes, can be used to climb to a road called Hauteville. Following this back down towards the town centre leads past Victor Hugo's house, where he lived in exile from France from 1855 to 1870. The uppermost room of **Hauteville House**, tel. 01481 721911, was Hugo's study, which enjoyed a view of his beloved France on a clear day. Further down the road is the National Trust of Guernsey Victorian Shop and Parlour, where Trust members may be in period costume.

St Peter Port Parish Church is generally referred to as the Town Church

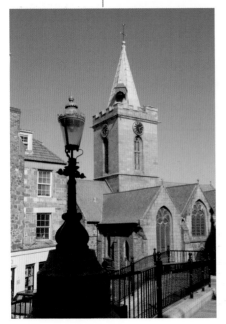

There is another opportunity to take a run at the shops along High Street, or you could follow the South Esplanade to Castle Pier. If you do go this way, watch out for a sculpture telling the story of Othon, a Swiss knight who was a great friend of Edward I, who was granted the Channel Islands for life in 1277. The sculpture is naturally beside the Credit Suisse offices!

Castle Pier has an upper walkway which can be used

to reach **Castle Cornet**, which has an entry charge, tel. 01481 721657. The castle grew on a rocky islet to defend St Peter Port and Guernsey. If the castle is visited, the rest of the day might quietly disappear as there is so much to see.

CASTLE CORNET

Castle Rock may have been inhabited by Neolithic and Bronze Age people, while Castle Cornet was developed almost as soon as King John lost Normandy to France in 1204. The French raided frequently in the 13th century, and in 1338 they took the castle and held it for seven years. The castle was considerably extended and strengthened in the 16th century, and later held out for nearly nine years as a Royalist stronghold in the 17th century when the rest of Guernsey supported Parliament in the Civil War.

A massive explosion occurred when the magazine in the central keep was struck by lightning in 1672, accounting for the rather squat form of the castle today. There were improvements to the fortifications in the 18th and 20th centuries, with concrete structures added during the German Occupation, augmenting the castle's ability to defend the harbour. The site

includes a number of small museums, including a maritime museum, and attractive little gardens add colour to the bare walls. Traditionally, a cannon is fired around noon each day from the ramparts.

Head back into town via the harbourside to return to the Liberation Monument.

Walking round St Peter Port early or late in the day is quite relaxing, and several pubs and restaurants offer a cosmopolitan range of food and drink. When there are fewer cars and people on the streets there is a chance to look at the finer detail of the buildings, spotting all sorts of interesting plaques and monuments telling more about the history of the place. ▶

There are sometimes guided heritage walks around town and the tourist information centre can provide details of any taking place during your visit.

WALK 2
St Peter Port and Fermain Bay

Distance	6.5km (4 miles)
Terrain	Good coastal and woodland paths, with plenty of steps up and down, and some road walking.
Start/Finish	Bus Station, St Peter Port
Refreshments	Plenty of choice around St Peter Port. Beach café at Fermain Bay. Hotel restaurants and a pub at Fermain.
Transport	All buses serve St Peter Port. Buses 5 and 5A (south), 6 and 6A (south) and 7 and 7A run along Fort Road in Fermain village.

One of the most popular walks on Guernsey runs from St Peter Port to Fermain Bay. Although short, there are lots of ascents and descents on flights of steps, with enough woodland to make it feel more like a jungle trek than a coastal walk. In spring there are lovely carpets of bluebells. Marker stones carved with place-names show the way to Fermain Bay, but beware of paths leading steeply down to beaches and bays, as it is usually necessary to climb back up afterwards. Coastal fortifications and other attractions can be explored from the start, and an inland route is used to return to St Peter Port.

Leave the bus station and follow the **South Esplanade** out of St Peter Port, passing the harbour and walking beside **Havelet Bay**. A minor road leaves the main road and follows the coast, passing a café; however, instead of following the road, walk along a path on a terrace just above it. The wooded slopes of La Vallette rise steeply, with informal flower arrangements and rampant vegetation along the way. Follow the road through a rocky cutting then get back onto the path. The entrance to La Vallette Underground Military Museum is passed, while at the end of the road another tunnel entrance leads into the **Guernsey Aquarium**, and there is another beach café.

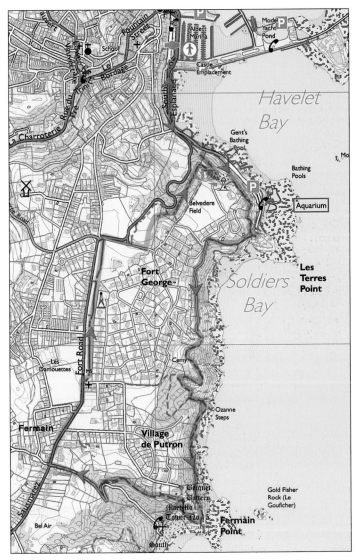

LA VALLETTE UNDERGROUND MILITARY MUSEUM

This series of tunnels was hacked out of tough gneiss during the German Occupation. The site was used primarily for storing fuel for U-boats, and an enormous fuel tank completely fills one tunnel. As a Military Museum, the tunnels are now filled with wartime memorabilia, including vehicles. There are coins, stamps and medals which were current during the Occupation, as well as some items from the First World War, and plenty of supporting literature is on sale. It is open daily March to mid-November, and there is an entry charge, tel. 01481 722300.

GUERNSEY AQUARIUM

A tunnel was constructed in 1864 to take a road from St Peter Port to Fermain Bay, but the scheme was abandoned at Soldiers Bay. During the German Occupation the old tunnel was strengthened and developed alongside the tunnels at La Vallette. A well-stocked aquarium now occupies the place, where 50 displays offer insights into local marine life, as well as more exotic species. Not only are fish displayed, but also a range of interesting amphibians. Fish and fish-keeping equipment are on sale too. Open daily all year, there is an entry charge, tel. 01481 723301.

Explore the fortifications, inspect the cannons and enjoy the views along the cliffs.

These woods are resplendent with bluebells in spring.

A long flight of steps climb above the aquarium, marked with a stone block indicating the cliff path to Fermain. At the top of the steps, Clarence Battery lies to the left on a rocky headland. ◀ Walk further uphill, still following stone markers across a wooded slope, passing above **Soldiers Bay**; the woodland path is often quite flowery. A left turn leads down a short road lined with a few houses at La Corniche.

Towards the end of the road the cliff path drifts left into woodland, with a wall alongside, and only odd glimpses of the sea. Turn right at a far corner of the wall and move inland into dense woods. Steps lead uphill, so keep left at two junctions to regain the cliff path. ◀ Flights of steps run downhill, while turning inland leads up to Fort Road, so keep an eye on the stone markers for Fermain Bay. The cliff path runs

Woodland paths are well-marked on the way to Fermain Bay and feature bluebells each spring

between fences, passing the **Ozanne Steps**. Do not go down this stout flight of steps, but walk across the slope, still watching for markers. A junction is reached where long flights of steps lead up and down; climb uphill and proceed with more open views. Take the second path on the left down into woodland, looking for another marker for Fermain Bay pointing left. ▶

To continue walking round the coast of Guernsey, refer to Walk 3.

The loopholed tower at **Fermain Bay** is also known as the Pepper Pot, and was one of a series of 15 towers built at strategic points around the coast between 1778 and 1780, of which 12 remain. Musket fire from the loopholes covered every possible approach, while a cannon could be fired from the roof. Loopholed towers gave way to Martello towers from 1794. There are a beach café and toilets beside the tower.

The route now heads inland, so retrace your steps back into the woods, looking for a stone carved with the words 'main road', with steps climbing from it. A well-wooded path climbs close to a couple of houses,

Pines tower over a grassy area beside Fort Road on the way from Fermain village to Fort George

then descends to the road serving Fermain Bay, near Le Chalet Hotel and the Fermain Valley Hotel. Follow the road, Fermain Lane, above these to reach the main road at **Fermain**, which is **Fort Road**.

Turn right to follow the road past the Fermain Tavern, leaving the village to pass the former Morley Methodist Church. A broad strip of grass forms a linear park beside the main road, with a path through it. Follow the path, noting the contrast between a number of huge pines and the tall masts of a Marine Radio Station. Turn right alongside a quiet road which runs towards an archway inscribed **Fort George**. Turn left downhill without passing through the arch, following a grassy path.

FORT GEORGE

As Castle Cornet's role in defending St Peter Port and Guernsey drew to a close in the 18th century, Fort George was raised above the town. Work on this extensive structure started in 1782 and continued for 20 years. Fort George became the main military headquarters for Guernsey and was continually improved throughout the 19th century. Dates over its gateways stretch from 1812 to 1845. During the German Occupation the fort was used as a military headquarters and its defences were strengthened. As a result, the site attracted Allied air raids. Little remains of the fort beyond its curtain wall, and the interior is now a housing estate.

The narrow grassy path along the foot of the wall becomes a broader woodland path, still following the wall, though the masonry is often obscured by ivy. The path follows an embankment parallel to the wall, reaching a viewpoint overlooking the harbour. Turn right, then left, away from a fine gateway and steps in the wall. A clear track runs downhill and, by keeping left, emerges from the woods and leads back onto the **South Esplanade** on the edge of St Peter Port.

WALK 3
Fermain and Jerbourg Point

Distance	10km (6¼ miles)
Terrain	Cliff and woodland paths, with plenty of steps up and down.
Start/Finish	Sausmarez Manor, Fermain
Refreshments	Cafés at Fermain Bay, Jerbourg Point and Moulin Huet Bay. Pub at Jerbourg.
Transport	Buses 5 and 5A (south), 6 and 6A (south) and 7 and 7A serve Fermain and Sausmarez Manor. Bus 6 (south) also serves Jerbourg.

A walk round rugged Jerbourg Point can be accomplished from Sausmarez Manor near Fermain. Fermain Bay is easily reached and a coastal path runs round to Petit Port and Moulin Huet Bay. Jerbourg Point is especially attractive when carpeted in flowers, with enough colour to distract attention from the concrete structures built during the German Occupation. The route can be varied in many places using a network of cliff and coastal paths. The inland stretch is quite short, including quiet roads and woodland paths.

A small part of **Sausmarez Manor** dates from the 13th century, and the de Sausmarez family has been associated with the place for eight centuries. Tours of the elegant house and its furnishings are available at certain times, and there is an entry charge. The grounds can be visited for free, where sculptures are dotted around. Other attractions incur entry charges, including subtropical gardens, a miniature railway and a pitch and putt course. A tearoom is available, as well as gift shops. The place is especially popular with families and regularly hosts events, including a Farmers' Market. Tel. 01481 235571. **www.sausmarezmanor.co.uk**.

Sausmarez Manor lies just outside the village of Fermain and could be visited at the start or finish of the walk. Follow the main road towards Fermain and St Peter Port then turn right as signposted for Del Mar Court. Keep left down the lane, crossing a stream at Le Varclin Abreuveur, then rise past the entrance to Del Mar Court. Follow the winding road until a sign indicates a left turn for Fermain Bay. A narrow, wooded road drops to a house called Fleur de Bois, where a sunken, stepped, woodland path continues downhill. At a junction near the sea, a left turn leads quickly to **Fermain Bay** and its beach café. However, if refreshment is not needed, turn right as marked by a stone block indicating St Martin's Point.

The rugged Pea Stacks lie off the end of Jerbourg Point and are a breeding ground for gulls

Climb a flight of steps on a wooded, flowery slope, with occasional views back to Fermain Bay and its prominent loopholed tower (see Walk 2). Keep climbing as marked for Calais and St Martin's Point. ▶ Plenty of steps lead up a bushy slope; then, when the path levels out a bit, keep straight ahead through junctions with other paths, following markers for St Martin's Point. The path rises, then steps to the left are marked for **Marble Bay** and St Martin's Point, leading down into a bushy valley. Cross the valley and climb a slope of bracken, brambles and flowers to pass through mixed woodlands planted with a number of tall pines.

The path network allows a variety of routes to be plotted; for instance, steps run downhill, marked for Bec du Nez and Marble Bay, which afford a view of a tiny jetty at La Divette.

Continue as marked for St Martin's Point. The trees thin out, there are fewer steps and the path undulates across the slope above the sea. Steps lead up onto a rocky ridge, and a left turn leads down a path beside a fence, out onto the rocky **St Martin's Point**. Concrete steps lead further down to an arch spanning a rocky chasm. A white cubic building can be reached, which houses a light and fog signal. Retrace your steps back across the arch and up along the rocky ridge, only this time keep climbing higher up a bushy slope to reach the Strassbourg Naval Battery Command Bunker at the top. ◄

A car park, food kiosk, toilets and Hotel Jerbourg lie just inland.

Strassbourg Naval Battery Command Bunker was constructed deep into the ground at Jerbourg during the German Occupation. It was bomb-proof and gas-proof, built to control huge guns mounted nearby. When the bunker was being built the nearby Doyle Monument was demolished. It was rebuilt in a smaller form after the war.

Follow a narrow road along the well-vegetated clifftop, then turn left along a path marked for Petit Port. A path on the left leads to an RSPB hide and it is worth having a look further downhill, as **Jerbourg Point** features plenty of flowers, and has amazing, jagged, rocky cliffs

Bel Air

Martello
Tower No. 5

**Fermain
Point**

South
Battery

*Fermain
Bay*

Calais

Courtes
Fallaizes

Route de Jerbourg

La Bouvée

Bec du
Nez
Battery

Bec du
Nez

*Le Pied
du Mur
(Marble Bay)*

Divette

Mount
Durand

P

Doyle
Column

PC

Moutonnière

*Petit
Port*

Jerbourg
Battery

PC

Jerbourg

La Moye
Battery

**St.
Martin's
Point**

*Vaux Bètes
(Telegraph
Bay)*

Les Tas de
Pois d'Amont
(Pea Stacks)

**Jerbourg
Point**

Les Grunes
de Jerbourg

49

The rugged Moulin Huet Bay, with the beach at Petit Port seen in the distance

and pinnacles not really appreciated from the higher paths. Retrace your steps and continue along the cliff-top path. Even if the diversion down the point is not taken, divert left down the next path, which at least gives a taste of how rugged the place is.

Jerbourg Point has a long history of settlement and defence. Neolithic people lived on the headland, and defensive ditches and mounds were in place by the Bronze Age. These structures were strengthened in medieval times, when the headland was a place of refuge for the islanders during frequent French raids. The stacks at the end of the point are the Pea Stacks, and the whole area is an important breeding ground for gulls.

Follow the path along the cliff top, which becomes quite bushy in places. There are good views around Petit Port and Moulin Huet Bay here. The path reaches a narrow tarmac road, which can be followed a little, or avoided by using narrow paths nearby. Either way, a path on left is marked for **Petit Port**, while just inland, near the **Doyle Monument**, is a pub called l'Auberge. Walk around rugged, flowery slopes, turning round a small, well-vegetated valley. ▸

If the path down to Petit Port is taken, retrace your steps to the cliff-top path. Short-cuts to Moulin Huet Bay depend on the tide being fully out.

After some gentle cliff-top walking, the path runs beside a wooded valley and reaches a road at Le Vallon. Turn left to reach a water trough, Courtes Fallaizes Abreuveur. Follow a clear path down through woods, beside a wall, and turn right round a corner of the wall. Follow the path through flowery woods to reach a road-end further down. A left turn leads down to a café and **Moulin Huet Bay**. ▸

To continue walking round the coast of Guernsey, pass the café and refer to Walk 4.

This route heads inland by following the road steeply up to a small car park and toilets. To the right is a marker stone for the Water Lanes. Follow this stone-paved path steeply up through the woods, with water babbling alongside. The path is deeply sunken and reaches a water trough and fine farm buildings at Ville Amphrey. Turn right along a narrow tarmac path between walls. This is the Ruette Fainel, leading to a fine old house decorated with coarse pieces of glassworks scrap. Note also the water-pump and stone troughs beside the house. Keep left to follow the driveway up through the gates then keep left again to follow a road uphill, passing houses and St Martin's Tennis Club.

At the top of the road, an old windmill tower lies to the left of a crossroads. The direction to walk, however, is to the right along a road, **Les Camps du Moulin**, marked 'no entry'. Walk straight through a skewed crossroads beside a shop to follow the busy Route de Sausmarez. This leads back to **Sausmarez Manor**, bus stops and the village of Fermain.

WALK 4

La Fosse and Icart Point

Distance	10km (6¼ miles)
Terrain	Rugged cliff coast walking, with several flights of steps. Easy woodland paths and gentle roads lead inland.
Start/Finish	Bella Luce Hotel, La Fosse
Refreshments	Hotel restaurants and cafés at Bella Luce, Moulin Huet Bay, Bon Port, Icart and Petit Bôt Bay.
Transport	Buses 6 and 6A (south) serve the Bella Luce Hotel and Icart.

This walk starts near Moulin Huet Bay, where buses pass the Bella Luce Hotel. Rugged bays and headlands flank Icart Point, so this walk features ever-changing views. The coastal path is popular and well-trodden, stretching from Moulin Huet Bay to Saints Bay and Icart Point, then round Le Jaonnet Bay to Petit Bôt Bay. Moving inland, a quiet path leads up through a well-wooded valley, then minor roads can be linked through La Villette and a *ruette tranquille* runs back to the Bella Luce Hotel.

The artist Renoir found inspiration here for 15 paintings during a month-long visit in 1883.

Buses do not run down the narrow road to Moulin Huet Bay, but pass the lovely **Bella Luce Hotel** at **La Fosse**. Walk down roads, first La Fosse du Bas, then Rue de Moulin Huet, and pass Moulin Huet Pottery. Further down the road is a small car park with toilets. Although a path is marked on the right for Saints Bay and Icart Point, it is worth going down to the end of the road, then down a narrow tarmac path past a café to **Moulin Huet Bay**. ◀ Just before the bay, a path heading right is marked for Saints Bay and Icart Point, crossing a little stream choked with Japanese knotweed.

Climb steps and turn left at a path junction. As a headland is turned above the Dog and Lion Rocks, Hotel **Bon Port** is a short way inland and offers refreshment if required. The cliff path is often enclosed by bushes, so coastal views are not always available. Head inland along the top of a well-wooded valley, keeping left to descend into it using a well-worn path. Turn left again down a road, then make a decision at a junction. Another left turn leads down a road to a kiosk and toilets at the head of **Saints Bay**, but a long climb is necessary to regain the cliff path. The road on the right serves Saint's Harbour, but watch for a flight of steps on the right, marked for Icart Point.

While climbing, views over the wooded valley take in a loopholed tower, Saints Bay and Saint's Harbour. Turn left at the top of the path, as marked for Icart Point. Note the steep path climbing from Saints Bay on the right. Don't just turn around **Icart Point** on the well-trodden path, but take time to walk out along the point too, enjoying the rocky, flowery headland and dramatic views. Not too far along the path is a road-end car park, where a café and toilets are hidden from sight.

Continue from the tearoom along a fine, flowery cliff path, reaching a junction beside a small stream. A left turn is marked for **Le Jaonnet Bay** only. ▶ Turn right to stay on the cliff-top path and enjoy views over the bay, as well as back to Icart Point. If the going gets tiring, an option to move inland is marked, otherwise cross a pronounced dip using steps which zigzag downhill then climb steeply. The path continues, turning right around a fence where stout pines are growing. The path winds down into a wooded valley and joins a road. A left turn leads quickly

A long descent on winding steps ends with a ladder down a cliff to reach a very rugged beach. Anyone going down must climb back afterwards!

A ladder-assisted descent to the rocky cove of Le Jaonnet Bay is an optional extra

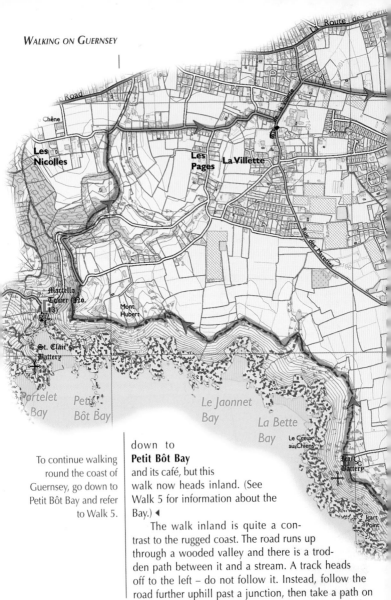

To continue walking round the coast of Guernsey, go down to Petit Bôt Bay and refer to Walk 5.

down to **Petit Bôt Bay** and its café, but this walk now heads inland. (See Walk 5 for information about the Bay.) ◄

The walk inland is quite a contrast to the rugged coast. The road runs up through a wooded valley and there is a trodden path between it and a stream. A track heads off to the left – do not follow it. Instead, follow the road further uphill past a junction, then take a path on

the left, immediately fording a small stream. The woodland path crosses a track and rises to a road. Turn right to follow the road through a shrubbery near some houses. Turn right along La Hurette Lane, rising from the wooded valley to pass a row of houses. Take the second road

on the left, passing some older stone houses at Les Martins, then again take the second road on the left, a busy one, to pass La Villette Hotel.

At a crossroads at **La Villette** Garage, turn right as signposted for Moulin Huet Pottery, along a ruette tranquille called La Rue des Escaliers. This narrow road passes a playground and runs through a patchwork landscape of fields and greenhouses. Go through

Following a sunken woodland path inland from Petit Bôt Bay

a crossroads, along Rue des Frênes, to reach St Martin's Parish Cemetery. A right turn leads back to bus stops near the **Bella Luce Hotel** at **La Fosse**.

WALK 5
Le Bourg and Pointe de La Moye

Distance	11km (7 miles)
Terrain	Rugged cliff paths, with plenty of steps in places. Easy road walking inland, sometimes along *ruettes tranquilles*.
Start/Finish	Le Bourg
Refreshments	Pub at Le Bourg, while cafés are available at Petit Bôt Bay and Le Gouffre.
Transport	Buses 7 and 7A serve Le Bourg and Les Bruliaux. Bus 4 also serves Le Bourg.

The coast from Petit Bôt Bay to Pointe de la Moye, Le Gouffre and La Corbière is quite adaptable as there are a number of spur paths that can be used, either to visit rugged headlands or divert inland early. Beyond La Corbière, there are plenty of steps up and down on the way to a prominent German observation tower at La Prévôte. A circular walk can be enjoyed by moving inland, and at the start/finish there is an opportunity to visit the German Occupation Museum near Ste Marguérite de la Forêt Parish Church.

Ste Marguérite de la Forêt, or Forest Church, stands on high ground that may once have been occupied by a dolmen, and some massive stones form the foundation of the church. The structure can be dated to the 13th century but it may be older, and there are 15th century extensions. It was completely restored in 1891. There is a peal of six bells and a collection of old musical instruments.

Start on the main road at Le Bourg, where Ste Marguérite de la Forêt Parish Church can be visited, and the **German Occupation Museum** is signposted. While following the road from the church to the museum, do not miss the delightful 'Rectory Wild Spot' on the right, where a wonderfully tangled mass of vegetation is served by a very short path.

GERMAN OCCUPATION MUSEUM

From the outside, where there is a mine and heavy artillery, the museum looks like a little cottage. Inside, there is a lot of space full of wartime memorabilia. There are video presentations and rooms devoted to military and civilian life during the German Occupation. Maps of Guernsey show the extent of a light railway system that was constructed from St Peter Port to St Sampson and round much of the north coast. Occupation Street is an interesting reconstruction of shop-fronts, and there is a fire engine and other large vehicles. The museum has plenty of literature and other items on sale, and incorporates a tearoom. There is an entry charge, tel. 01481 238205.

Leave the museum and turn right down the road. Turn sharply right and left to pass a former hotel, The Manor. The road can be followed straight down to Petit Bôt Bay, but there is a better approach. Turn left to cross a footbridge and follow a clear woodland path, contouring and climbing, with one good view down to the bay. The path joins a track, which leads down to a road. Turn right down the road, or use a path alongside it, to reach **Petit Bôt Bay**.

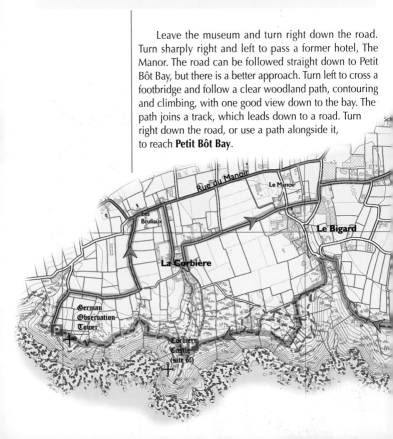

The head of the lovely **Petit Bôt Bay** has what appears to be a stout, stone sea wall. In fact it is an old dam, which once impounded water flowing down the wooded valley to provide power for a mill. Another mill higher up the valley was demolished during the German Occupation, and water was used to generate electricity at the lower mill. The dam has been filled and the mill is now a café, but the stream still runs beneath the building.

Follow the road around the café, as if climbing back inland, but turn left up a flight of steps marked for

59

St Clair's Battery features a magazine, paved battery platform and good views back to Petit Bôt Bay.

Portelet and Le Gouffre. On the way up the steps, consider making a detour down to the left where another flight of steps is marked 'Battery'. ◀ Note also a path marked for Portelet, but taking either detour requires more effort and the retracing of steps. If these detours are not taken, then keep to the path marked for Le Gouffre, which becomes enclosed by bushes with only a few views of the sea. A short path on the left leads to an old watch house hidden among bushes. After passing a house, follow a broad track onwards, flanked by gorse and other bushes, turning into a wooded valley with views ahead to Pointe de la Moye.

A road leads straight inland to the airport, offering a short-cut, passing Les Caches Farm on the left, beautifully restored and thatched in 2007 by the National Trust of Guernsey.

A path to the left of the track turns around the head of the wooded valley near **Les Fontenelles**. Emerge from the trees with a clearer view of the point and the twisting fishermen's path it supports. Steps wind down towards **Pointe de la Moye**, and it looks as if there is no option but to go all the way down to the sea, but a right turn reveals a broad track. This rises gradually across a rugged slope and turns inland to reach **Le Gouffre**, where there is a café and a gift shop. ◀

Looking westwards along the cliffs after leaving the German observation tower at La Prévôte

Climb the steps beside the café, and then the path rises between bushes. A detour to the left is signed to Les Herbeuses viewpoint. This is worth taking for the view it offers back to Pointe de la Moye, but return to the main cliff path to continue. The path reaches a house, where a track and road lead inland at **Le Bigard**. Keep left at a road junction and make a sharp left turn along a track marked for La Corbière, crossing National Trust of Guernsey property. Follow this track, but feel free to use of any paths branching left from it. An area of bracken and gorse scrub features a network of paths offering good views of the cliffs. A small car park is reached at **La Corbière**, where a diversion inland could bring the walk to an early finish.

Follow the path marked for La Prévôte and Pleinmont Point. At first the path looks as if it is heading for the end of the point, but it swings right down a steep flight of steps. ▸ More steps climb uphill, then down, then up, making this a roller-coaster route. It could prove energy-sapping for anyone trying to cover a long stretch of the coastal path. Eventually, a prominent **German observation tower** is reached at La Prévôte, with a small car park beyond. ▸

Resist the temptation to short-cut too early down to the right.

To continue walking round the coast of Guernsey, refer to Walk 6.

LA PRÉVÔTE GERMAN OBSERVATION TOWER

Although Le Hâvre de Bon Repos looks completely rock-bound, there is a landing point and successive lookouts have been built here. An 18th century watch house was built in response to a threat of invasion by Napoleonic forces. The German observation tower is altogether more substantial – a huge, concrete cylinder with narrow slits where range-finding equipment was located. Almost all the German fortifications on the Channel Islands were built by the navy, but this one was built by the army. Although it dominates the cliffs at La Prévôte, the structure hardly compares with the enormous towers further westwards, visited on Walks 6 and 7.

Walk along the road, turning right and left to reach the main road at **Les Bruliaux**. Turn right and within a short distance turn right again, as marked for La Corbière.

The German Occupation Museum near Le Bourg is well worth exploring at the start or finish of the walk

Follow the road, a ruette tranquille, along, downhill and to the left, then turn left and climb steeply from a junction at **La Corbière**. The road later turns right and runs straight through the countryside, passing houses. Avoid a road to the left, pass the fine stone building of La Carrière, then go down through a crossroads and uphill.

Turn left uphill at a junction at Les Merriennes, then turn right along a tree-lined road. Keep straight ahead past houses, and go straight through a crossroads near a Baptist Chapel. The road runs straight towards Ste Marguérite de la Forêt and the main road at **Le Bourg**. There are buses, a pub, a shop and access to all the facilities at the nearby airport too.

WALK 6

La Prévôte and Torteval

Distance	10km (6¼ miles)
Terrain	Rugged cliff paths, quiet roads and a few paths and tracks inland.
Start/Finish	Les Bruliaux
Refreshments	None on the route, but a pub is available at nearby Portelet Harbour.
Transport	Buses 7 and 7A serve Les Bruliaux and Portelet Harbour, and run close to St Philippe de Torteval. Buses 4, 5 and 5A (south) run close to St Pierre du Bois.

A fine stretch of cliff coast path stretches from La Prévôte to Mont Hèrault, linking a German observation tower with an older watch house. Fine cliff views can be enjoyed along the way. Afterwards, it is worth moving inland on quiet roads to visit a couple of interesting churches: St Philippe de Torteval and St Pierre du Bois. There are opportunities to see how varied the land use and housing styles are in south-west Guernsey. Several minor roads are followed through the countryside, as well as field paths and tracks, which are relatively rare around Guernsey.

Start at **Les Bruliaux**, where a minor road is marked 'To La Prévôte Watch Tower'. Follow the road towards cliffs, ending at a small car park just below the **German**

Looking back along the cliffs to the German observation tower at La Prévôte

63

observation tower at La Prévôte. Turn right to follow the cliff path, which is marked for Pleinmont Point. Drop down steps, then climb, then follow the path in a roller-coaster fashion with flowery banks and fine views along the cliffs. Along the way, two marker stones indicate paths running inland to the main road. One is a National Trust of Guernsey path and the

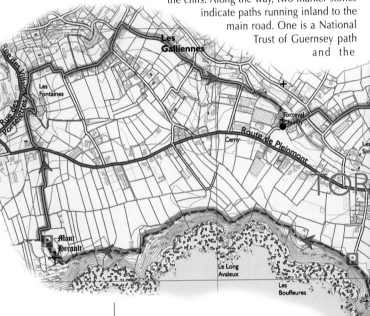

Note the pointed rocks at the base of the cliff.

other is at the head of a little valley at **Le Creux Mahie**. ◄ Later, a short spur path to the left leads to a battery platform above **Les Tielles**, which is another fine viewpoint. The main cliff path emerges from bushes to pass an abundance of flowers, with fleshy, creeping mesembryanthemum swathing the cliffs near a small car park.

The path continues, marked for Mont Hèrault and Pleinmont Point, and is much easier. There are views inland of patchwork fields, and the spire of Torteval Church is a good reference point, seen often during the

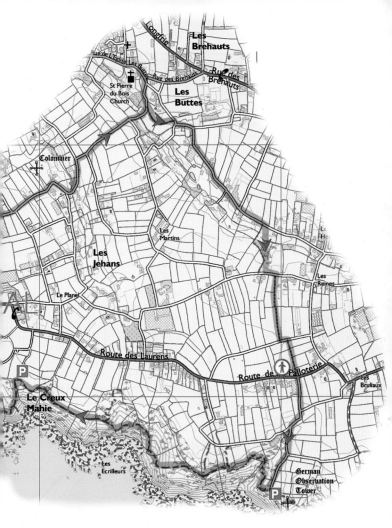

course of the walk. The cliff scenery is very dramatic and one rocky headland is pierced with an arch. After a bushy stretch, the path runs close to **Mont Hèrault Watch House**, which can be approached by making a short detour. ▸

To continue walking round the coast of Guernsey, refer to Walk 7.

MONT HÈRAULT WATCH HOUSE

This was one of several observation posts and signalling points erected against the threat of French invasion before and during the Napoleonic wars. During the latter part of the 18th century these sites were manned by the Guernsey Militia. The approach of enemy shipping was conveyed to the military headquarters at Fort George by a chain of beacons erected along the coast. The neighbouring Pleinmont Watch House featured as a haunted house in Victor Hugo's *Les Travailleurs de Mer* but was demolished during the German Occupation.

Follow a track and road inland from the watch house to reach the main road at **Les Fontaines**. Cross over the main road and follow a narrower road winding downhill, passing a number of houses in a little valley. Just before reaching the main road again, turn right and climb up another narrow road marked with a 'steep hill' sign. ◀ Turn left at a junction, then follow the road to another junction at a house called Vue des Étoiles, and keep left. Turn right along another road, rising to spot the tall and slender spire of Torteval Church in the distance.

The main road could be followed down to Portelet Harbour, where there is a pub.

Simply follow the road towards the spire. Some fine granite houses are couched in a dip, where you walk straight through a crossroads and climb uphill. When the road runs downhill and turns sharply left, keep straight ahead along a narrow road marked as 'no through road'. This is a lovely, leafy *ruette tranquille* which leads straight to **St Philippe de Torteval**. Follow the churchyard wall round to find the main entrance to the church, and take a look inside.

Although **St Phillipe de Torteval Parish Church** was built in 1818, it stands close to the site of a much earlier church, which was demolished in 1816. The round tower and slender spire ensure that this church is unlikely to be confused with any other church on Guernsey in distant views. One of the bells was cast in 1432 and is reckoned to be the oldest remaining church bell in the Channel Islands.

Follow the road downhill from the main entrance to the church, passing a water-pump and trough, then walk up through a staggered crossroads. The road bends right, then you turn left at a junction. Follow the road through mixed countryside, with fields, glasshouses and all types of dwelling houses. Go straight through another staggered crossroads and downhill. ▶ Keep to the left as the road drops and climbs. Turn right on the ascent at Les Falles, then keep left to approach the square stone tower of St Pierre du Bois. There is a dip in the road and the final climb is quite steep. The church is surrounded by some fine buildings, and there are toilets beside the Salle Paroissiale.

Note the cylindrical stone tower behind Le Colombier Farm.

St Pierre du Bois Parish Church is situated on sloping ground, and on entering the building, the slope is very evident along the floor. Although the church was mentioned as early as 1030, the present building was

St Pierre du Bois church is built on a slope and the floor inside also slopes noticeably

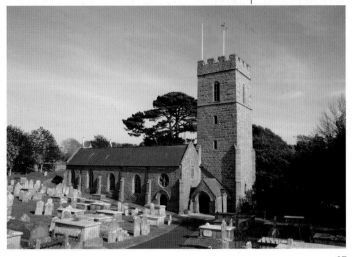

constructed in the 14th century and developed in the 15th century. The stout square tower holds 13 bells, which is the largest peal of bells in the Channel Islands.

Have a look round the church then retrace your steps back down the road. As the road begins to drop steeply, turn left along a pleasant path at **Les Buttes**, reaching a road junction and facing a house. Turn left up a road, facing the lights that guide aircraft towards the airport runway. Turn right up another road, passing La Fosse Farm. Note a road running left but do not follow that road; rather, keep straight ahead past a house called Le Pré. Turn right down a leafy path which crosses a little valley. The path is quite narrow and deeply sunk, and if there has been rain, it will be quite wet. Turn left along a road at the top, then turn right along a fine track to continue through fields. At the next road, turn left and almost immediately right along another narrow path. At the next road, the main road at **Les Bruliaux**, the walk ends exactly where it started.

A roadside stall offers a selection of vegetables

WALK 7

Portelet Harbour and Pleinmont

Distance	5km (3 miles)
Terrain	Quiet roads and rugged cliff paths.
Start/Finish	Portelet Harbour
Refreshments	Pub and café at Portelet Harbour.
Transport	Buses 7 and 7A serve Portelet Harbour.

The Pleinmont peninsula is at the extreme south-western end of Guernsey. The walk around it is quite popular and the area is riddled with paths. The route is circular, involving a short road walk inland before following a cliff path round the coast. There are several lookouts and fortifications, ranging from small coastal batteries to big German bunkers and a huge observation tower. The cliff scenery is dramatic and there is an abundance of flowers and shrubs along the way. This is also a great place for bird watching, with over 150 species recorded.

Start at the Imperial Hotel at **Portelet Harbour**, and follow the main road uphill and inland. On the ascent, take the second narrow road off to the left, then keep to the right to follow it further uphill. It simply offers an alternative ascent to the main road at **Les Fontaines**, and while it is just as bendy, it is unlikely to carry traffic. At the top walk straight across the main road to continue along another narrow road. This runs through fields and at its end there are tracks branching left and right. The one running left leads to the **Mont Hèrault Watch House** (see Walk 6 for information) which is worth a quick visit, but retrace your steps afterwards and walk along the other track. The cliff path continues down steps, rises and descends again. Eyes are likely to be fixed on a huge tower ahead, but look down into the cliff-girt inlet of **La Congrelle** first, then climb to the **German Observation Tower**.

Continue along the cliff-top and note the lime-stained Gull Rock out to sea. There are more steps across

69

a dip in the path; later there is a concrete bunker beside a car park. Further along the path, a circular German gun emplacement is passed, part of the extensive 'Batterie Dollmann'. Far out to sea, the slender Hanois Lighthouse may be seen, usually omitted from maps of Guernsey. The cliff path passes gorse and brambles enlivened

by flowery areas. The ruins of the **Pleinmont Watch House** are passed, and the path runs easily over high ground from another little car park. A prominent mast is passed and the Pleinmont Observation Tower looms very large. If this is visited it is best approached by road from the next car park.

GERMAN OBSERVATION TOWERS

The south-western end of Guernsey was well fortified during the German Occupation. Massive concrete towers housed range-finding equipment and calculations were made to enable huge guns to fire shells far out to sea. The bunkers and gun emplacements of Batterie Dollmann are still quite obvious between two prominent observation towers. The Pleinmont Observation Tower has limited opening times – usually Wednesday and Sunday from April to October, and just Sunday in winter. Members of the Channel Islands Occupation Society, www.occupied. guernsey.net, are available at those times to help visitors explore the site.

A marker indicates the path to Portelet, and a little further ahead another marker points left down a flight of steps. ▶ The coastal scenery is charming, but stop at an old battery platform and have a look at the paths criss-crossing all around, to decide which ones to follow. Basically, aim for a road-end, but on the way, notice La Table des Pions, which is a circular structure in a grassy area. Before following the road, visit **Fort Pezeries**, which is a stout little battery on a rugged headland.

Staying high leads into a maze of bushy and wooded paths, well worth exploring some other time.

La Table des Pions, a curious earthwork and circle of stones, looks prehistoric, but may be only a few centuries old. It was a traditional resting and feasting place used on a three-yearly basis during inspections of Guernsey's coastal roads and sea defences. Legends have grown up around La Table, stating that the circular groove was worn bare by fairies dancing around the stone circle all night!

The star-shaped **Fort Pezeries** was built to cover the defence of the southern part of Rocquaine Bay. It was founded around 1680 and further augmented in the 18th century. During the German Occupation it was not developed as brutally as the rest of the Pleinmont peninsula. Views from the fort extend around Rocquaine Bay to Fort Grey, Fort Saumarez and Lihou Island.

To continue walking round the coast of Guernsey, refer to Walk 8.

Follow the road round the rugged bay, noticing a concrete tunnel while rising round a headland. There is one short stretch of grassy path beside the road, but in any case the road is generally barred to traffic. In fact, coastal erosion has weakened the road in places, so eventually it may be lost to the sea. A café and toilets are passed before the road leads back to the Imperial Hotel and bus stop at **Portelet Harbour**. ◀

Cannons point seawards from the battery at the star-shaped Fort Pezeries

WALK 8
Rocquaine Bay and Lihou Island

Distance	6.5km (4 miles)
Terrain	Mostly road or beach walking, depending on the tide. The extension to Lihou Island is dependent upon the state of the tide.
Start	Portelet Harbour
Finish	L'Erée
Refreshments	Pubs and cafés are available at Portelet Harbour and L'Erée. Guernsey Pearl, near Fort Grey, also has a restaurant.
Transport	Buses 7 and 7A serve Portelet Harbour. Buses 5 and 5A (south), 7 and 7A serve Fort Grey and L'Erée.

This walk is linear, ending with a short loop around an interesting wetland area featuring a profusion of wild flowers and waterfowl. There are two ways to walk round Rocquaine Bay, depending on the state of the tide. If the tide is in, then there is no option but to follow a busy road that does not always have a pavement. If the tide is out, then a fine sandy beach is available. The walk is short, but there are several points of interest along the way. An optional extension to the island of Lihou is possible, but only at low water during spring tides.

Start at **Portelet Harbour**, where the Imperial Hotel over-looks the sea. If the tide is in and beating against the sea wall, then follow the main road around Rocquaine Bay, taking care where there is no pavement. If the tide is out, then walk on the sandy beach below the sea wall. There are steps and slipways allowing walkers to switch between the beach and the road on the way to **Fort Grey**. ▶

Other attractions nearby include Guernsey Pearl, the Green Island Centre and a café.

FORT GREY SHIPWRECK MUSEUM

Fort Grey is a Martello tower, built in 1804, standing within an older circular battery on the site of the former Rocquaine Castle. It is known locally as the Cup and Saucer, and a stout causeway allows it to be reached at ▶

Fort Grey Shipwreck Museum can be reached by a stout causeway at any state of the tide

any state of the tide. The museum's upper gallery is devoted to navigation and has plenty of information about the Hanois Lighthouse. The lower gallery is devoted to shipwrecks and marine archaeology. A grassy area surrounds the Martello tower, where a cannon points out to sea. There are two magazines – one inside the battery and another outside. Open daily from March to October, there is an entry charge, tel. 01481 265036, www.museums.gov.gg.

Continue along the road or the beach, bearing in mind that steps and slipways allow walkers to switch between one and the other. Whichever route is used, German concrete bunkers guard the middle of Rocquaine Bay, contrasting with the fine stonework of the sea wall. The top of the bunkers may be remarkably flowery. ◀ Continue past **La Saline**; further round the bay a concrete promenade path parts company with the main road at **L'Erée**, where options for food and drink include a hotel bar, cafés and a tea garden operated by La Société Guernsiaise, www.societe.org.gg. The tea garden also offers information about the natural history of the area.

Walk 19 starts here, exploring the countryside inland from the bay.

There are toilets available and another German bunker lies at the end of the promenade. Across the road a large field was once used as an airfield before the development of Guernsey Airport. The field was later saved from building development and is now the **Colin Best Nature Reserve**.

Map continues on page 77

The walk around the bay is complete, but explorations continue onto the next headland, following a road to signposted for Lihou Island. Do not be tempted to follow what looks like a good coastal path, since this ends abruptly, and in any case the road passes a fine dolmen at **Le Creux ès Faïes**, which should not be missed.

Le Creux ès Faïes, an impressive Neolithic passage tomb, was built around 3000–2500BC and was used until the Late Bronze Age, around 1000BC. The chamber is large enough to stand up in and was used for burials over many centuries. The kerbstones have been repositioned and the chamber is completely covered by a huge mound. According to legend, the passage was the entrance to Fairyland. Soldiers stationed at Fort Saumarez used the place as a hideout while sleeping off hangovers, so for a time the chamber was filled with rubble to deter them!

Continue to a car park on a flowery headland, where L'Erée Point Battery can be inspected. The road ends at a sign offering advice about visiting **Lihou Island**, but this is

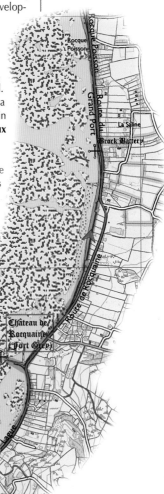

75

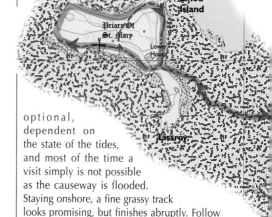

optional,
dependent on
the state of the tides,
and most of the time a
visit simply is not possible
as the causeway is flooded.
Staying onshore, a fine grassy track
looks promising, but finishes abruptly. Follow
a narrow path uphill beside a fence, then weave
through defensive trenches near a prominent observation tower before walking down to a road junction. Turn
left to walk down past **Fort Saumarez**, reaching the main
coastal road.

> **Fort Saumarez** features an 18th century battery, with
> a Martello tower added in 1804. During the German
> Occupation a tall observation tower was built on top

*During the German
Occupation, a Martello
tower at Fort Saumarez
was capped by an
observation tower*

of the Martello tower. Parts of the fort can be seen from nearby paths and roads, but the site is a private dwelling surrounded by luxuriant gardens.

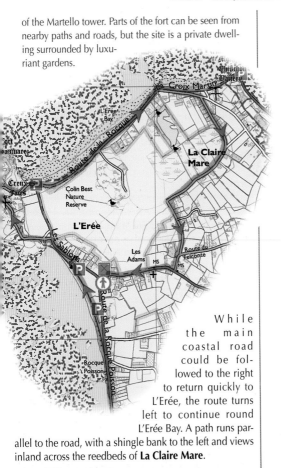

While the main coastal road could be followed to the right to return quickly to L'Erée, the route turns left to continue round L'Erée Bay. A path runs parallel to the road, with a shingle bank to the left and views inland across the reedbeds of **La Claire Mare**.

L'ERÉE SHINGLE BANK AND LA CLAIRE MARE

The shingle bank around L'Erée Bay protects La Claire Mare and between them is a variety of habitats. The shingle bank is an important nesting place for birds and also features plants adapted to dry stony conditions. The wetlands ▶

of La Claire Mare are protected as a nature reserve and attract waders and waterfowl, with warblers frequenting the reed beds. Gulls and herons are also present, along with piping curlew. Further away from the water, the meadows are often ablaze with wild flowers, including several species of orchid.

To continue walking round the coast of Guernsey, stay on the main road and refer to Walk 9.

The path beside the shingle bank rejoins the main road at a slipway. Lying offshore is a scrap of grass known as La Capelle, or Chapelle Dom Hué, which was once inhabited by a hermit. A patchy narrow road runs parallel to the main road just inland at La Rocque. Turn right at a junction to walk inland. ◄

A rugged headland at the western end of Lihou Island, reached by an optional tidal extension

The road heading inland passes between houses and then turns right around a low-lying area. Reed beds and the small pool of **La Claire Mare** are seen, surrounded by flowery meadows. The road later turns left uphill, but keep right at the next two junctions. Les Adams Methodist Church is passed on the way back to the main coastal road at **L'Erée**.

Optional Extension to Lihou Island

Lihou Island is reached by a tidal causeway, and a notice offers advice to visitors, listing the safe times that the causeway can be used. 'Time and tide waits for no man', as the saying goes, and most of the time the causeway is underwater, so this walk is only possible at low water during spring tides. The cobbled causeway crosses low-lying granite and shingle, coming ashore on Lihou Island at a large notice explaining about the Lihou Island Reserve. Follow a path to the left of Lihou House and its walled enclosure. The path passes the ruins of a Benedictine Priory, where bracken gives way to grassy and flowery ground. Turn round the end of the island, noting Lihoumel Island, an important bird reserve. The path rises above outcrops of granite and passes through a low ruined wall. Another wall is passed later and the path returns to the house and causeway. Retrace your steps back across the causeway. This extension measures 3km (2 miles) there and back.

LIHOU ISLAND

The Benedictine Priory of Notre Dame de Lihou dates from at least 1156 and was a dependency of Mont St Michel in France. It was confiscated in 1414 and granted to Eton College, and ceased to be a religious house in the 16th century. It was unfortunately used for target practice in both the Napoleonic and Second World Wars. Lihou House is 19th century, but has been rebuilt in recent years, and can be hired by groups.

There are two important breeding sites for seabirds, the Lissroy shingle bank and Lihoumel Island. Flowery grasslands are noted for their carpets of thrift and autumn squill. There are around 100 species of bird, 120 species of plant and 130 species of seaweed around the island. The shore and sea surrounding the island is a Ramsar reserve.

WALK 9

Perelle Bay and St Saviour

Distance	11km (7 miles)
Terrain	Low-level coastal walking, mostly quiet roads inland with a few paths and tracks.
Start/Finish	La Rocque
Refreshments	Hotel restaurant at Perelle, a café at Vazon and a pub near St Saviour's Parish Church.
Transport	Buses 7 and 7A serve the coast road between Le Trépied and Vazon. Bus 5 (south) passes St Apolline's Chapel.

A simple coastal walk round Perelle Bay, Richmond and Vazon can be extended inland to St Saviour's Parish Church and St Saviour's Reservoir. The reservoir is the largest on Guernsey and a shoreline path was established in 2000 as a Millennium Walk. St Saviour's Church and the tiny St Apolline's Chapel both have very long histories and are both are worth visiting. Hidden beneath St Saviour's Church is a network of tunnels, dug during the German Occupation. This walk is very varied, with several points of interest and the scenery seems to change with every turn on the road.

Either look at Le Trépied Dolmen straight away, or wait until the end of the walk.

Start on the main coastal road at La Rocque. ◀ Following the road round **Perelle Bay** is awkward as there is not always a pavement. The beach can be used at low water, but it is very rocky. There are steps and slipways along the sea wall allowing walkers to switch between the road and beach. There is a garage shop at Perelle, followed by a hotel called L'Atlantique. A pebbly and sandy beach continues onwards, and the **Perelle Battery**, locally known as Le Bas Marais, overlooks the middle of the bay. At the end of the bay a slipway links the road and the beach at **Richmond**, where a decision needs to be made.

There is no coastal path or coastal road, so if the tide is in the main road must be followed straight to Vazon Bay. If the tide is out the beach is very rocky, but it can be followed round a headland. **Fort Richmond**, a squat, square 19th century structure, can be seen but

not approached. The end of the headland is covered in masses of tall umbellifers, and it is possible to step ashore for a while. Just a little inland there are two menhirs on a private driveway near the site of **Fort le Crocq**. The cobbly beach gets much easier underfoot and a minor road leads onto the main coastal road.

Vazon Bay features a fine crescent of firm sand at low tide, with low outcrops of rock, and plenty of wading birds can be spotted. A path runs along the top of a sea wall, flanked by tall flowers. The Richmond Kiosk offers food and drink half-way round the bay, with a concrete bunker and toilets alongside. A little further along, Rue du Gele heads inland at Vazon. ▶ Follow **Rue du Gele** straight inland until the road bends left at a large water trough. At this point, turn right up a *ruette tranquille*, passing a landscaped outcrop of rugged gneiss. At the top of the road, make a quick left and right turn through a staggered crossroads, climbing steeply up another ruette tranquille. The road runs through an area of high fields where there are no houses, which is unusual in Guernsey. Turn left at the top of Ruette du Haut Sejours to walk along Rue des Hougues. Turn right at a crossroads to walk down a busier road, then climb uphill past a monumental

Walkers trying to avoid the road around Perelle Bay might find the shore rather too rocky in places

To continue walking round the coast of Guernsey, stay on the main coastal road to pass La Grande Mare Hotel, and refer to Walk 10.

stone water trough, dated 1898, at **Les Lohiers**. A road on the left leads to La Grande Lande Vinery; however, keep straight ahead and later turn right towards **St Saviour's Parish Church**, where a path can be followed into the churchyard.

The hilltop site of **St Saviour's Parish Church** probably had some religious significance before the church was built. An ancient menhir in the churchyard has a deeply inscribed cross upon it. The church is a notable landmark, being large and situated on an elevated position. The site was a gift from Duke Robert of Normandy to the Benedictines of Mont St Michel in Normandy in 1030. Parts of the building date from the 12th century and most of it dates from the 14th and 15th centuries. The tower was

destroyed by lightning and had to be rebuilt in 1658. During the German Occupation the tower was used as an observation post, while tunnels were dug beneath the churchyard.

There are three ways to leave the churchyard. Don't leave via the main entrance, but consider one of the other two paths. One descends past a hut, crossing a road at **Sous l'Église**, which can be used if you are in a hurry. The other path is stone-paved, leading to a road junction beside the Auberge du Val Hotel and its delightful herb gardens. By turning left up a minor road at this junction, the entrance to St Saviour's Tunnels can be seen.

Map continues on page 84

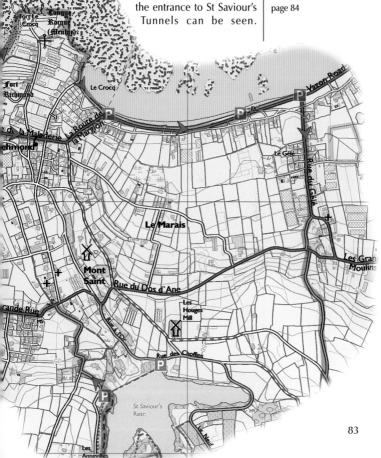

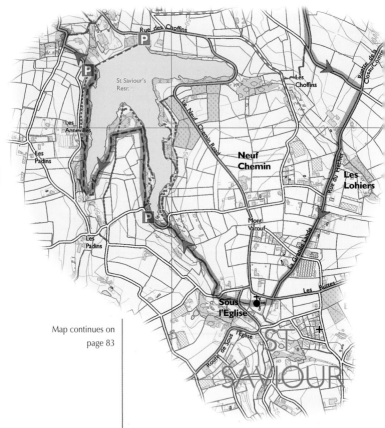

Map continues on
page 83

Afterwards, either walk back up to the churchyard and
take the other path downhill, or take a short-cut straight
up the road to **Sous l'Église**.

St Saviour's Tunnels beneath St Saviour's Church
were built during the German Occupation, hacked
from tough gneiss by slave workers brought in by
Organisation Todt. At the end of the Occupation the
tunnels were used as a dump for a huge amount of

military equipment. Later, the site was opened as a visitor attraction, until the roof caved in, and it has been closed ever since. There were fears that subsidence could damage the church.

A path leaves the road at **Sous l'Église**, passing a house and descending through woods. Turn left along a road, then right to follow a narrow path beside a house. This path is mostly tree-lined, with flowery banks, proceeding through a grassy or wooded valley. ▶ Turn left along another road, climbing a little and watching for a gate on the right. A well-wooded path runs alongside St Saviour's Reservoir, but the trees are so dense that very little is seen of the water. The path runs almost to the end of a peninsula jutting into the reservoir, but turns left to cut across it. Cross a footbridge over an inflowing stream and walk along the western shore of the reservoir, seeing more of the water on the way to the dam and a car park.

> There is a swampy section in the middle of the valley, but the path itself is usually fairly dry.

St Saviour's Reservoir is the largest reservoir on Guernsey. Construction began in 1938 but was interrupted by the German Occupation and it was not completed until 1947. It is frequented by a variety of ducks and waders, and well used by trout fishermen. Kingfishers may sometimes be seen, while firecrests and flycatchers find the conifers along the shore particularly attractive. The path making a circuit all the way round the convoluted shore of the reservoir is called the Millennium Walk and it was opened in the year 2000.

Exit onto a minor road and turn right. Keep right as the road, a ruette tranquille, descends to a busy road near **Mont Saint**. The busy road is La Grande Rue. Turn left to follow it past the United Reformed Church to reach **St Apolline's Chapel**. This ancient roadside chapel is well worth a quick visit.

The little **St Apolline's Chapel** dates from at least the 1390s and was originally La Chapelle de Ste Marie de Perelle. A local legend explains how it became St

Apolline's. The Seigneur's wife was tired of losing two teeth for every pregnancy she endured, and fearing the loss of two more on her fifth confinement, she made a vow to St Apolline, patron saint of dentists. Not only was she spared the loss of her teeth, but all her lost ones were miraculously restored, so the chapel was dedicated to St Apolline! The building has been beautifully restored, with great care taken over ancient frescoes on the walls and ceiling.

At the end of the road, the walk could be cut short by turning right for **Perelle**, but if there is time, it is worth extending the walk a little. Turn left uphill at the end of La Grande Rue, as marked for L'Erée. Turn right at a crossroads near the top, and immediately right again past La Hure Cottage. A lovely ruette rises between a concrete bunker and Le Catioroc. The path leads from a wooded area to an open, grassy National Trust of Guernsey property. Follow the path onwards to inspect Le Trépied Dolmen (if not done already) and **Mont Chinchon Battery**, finishing on the main coastal road below at La Rocque.

Le Trépied Dolmen is a Neolithic chambered tomb built around 3000–2500BC and was in use until the Late Bronze Age, around 1000BC. No trace of a mound or kerbstones remains. In the 17th century the place was repeatedly mentioned during witch trials. Guernsey witches were said to have been joined by fairy folk from nearby Le Creux ès Faïes, chanting slogans against the priory on Lihou Island. Friday night sabbats were allegedly attended by the Devil himself.

The adjacent **Mont Chinchon Battery** was also known as the Druid's Altar Battery because of its location beside Le Trépied Dolmen.

WALK 10
Vazon Bay and Cobo Bay

Distance	9.5km (6 miles)
Terrain	Easy coastal paths, followed by paths, tracks and roads inland.
Start/Finish	La Grande Mare Hotel, Vazon Bay
Refreshments	Cafés at Vazon Bay, pubs and cafés at Cobo.
Transport	Buses 3, 3A, 7 and 7A serve Vazon and Cobo. Buses 5 and 5A serve King's Mills.

The coastal walk from Vazon Bay to Cobo Bay is quite easy. It starts with a simple promenade walk then wanders round a headland dominated by Fort Hommet. Easy coastal paths and road-walking lead round to Cobo Bay. The climb onto a fine rocky viewpoint at Le Guet should not be missed in clear weather. Quiet roads and a few little paths allow the walk to proceed inland, exploring some of the more rural parts of Guernsey.

Vazon Bay was the site of an invasion in 1372, when Owen Lawgoch of Wales, known as Yvon de Galles to Guernsey folk, landed a Welsh and Aragonese force with French backing and subdued the whole of Guernsey. This was intended to be the first step to claiming the throne of Wales, but he left the island at the request of Charles V of France to join other offensives around Europe.

La Grande Mare Hotel is set back from the head of Vazon Bay, almost surrounded by a **golf course**. Either walk along a sandy beach when the tide is out, or follow a promenade path between the beach and the coastal road. ▶ A prominent loopholed tower sits on the promenade, flanked by German bunkers and an old magazine building. The Vazon Bay Beach Café and toilets are passed, while Crabby Jack's offers food and drink across the road.

There are opportunities to switch between the beach and promenade.

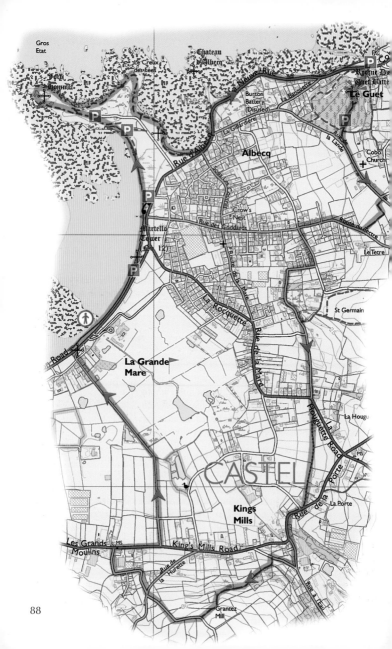

Gros
Etat

Château d'Albecq

Le Creux
des Fees

PC

Rocque Du
Guet Batte

Fort
Hommet

Nouvelle Rue

Le Guet

Burton
Battery
(Disused)

La Bandierie

La Garderie

La Lande

Rue d'Albecq

Albecq

La Rousee

Cobo
Church

Rue des Paddards

Crow's
Nest

Route du Becco

Le Tetre

Martello
Tower
(No. 12)

Rue de la Mare

La Rocquette

St Germain

Rond...

La Grande
Mare

Rue de la Mare

La Hougu...

Houguette Road

CASTEL

La Porte

Kings
Mills

Rue de la Porte

Les Grands
Moulins

MS

King's Mills Road

Rue de la Hurette

Rue d'Tel...

Grantez
Mill

The main road makes a short-cut straight to Cobo Bay, so stay on the promenade path. Follow a footpath away from a bunker at the end of the sea wall onto the Hommet headland. This is grassy and flowery, and there is a restored German gun casemate. Opening times are limited, but at those times members of the Channel Islands Occupation Society, www.occupied.guernsey.net, show visitors around. A clear path leads to **Fort Hommet**.

Fort Hommet stands on a rocky islet of pink Cobo Granite, joined to Guernsey by a belt of sand dunes. Habitat types include dunes, heath, wet meadow and salt marsh. There are traces of settlement from the Neolithic and Iron Ages, while a medieval settlement site lies near Albecq, dating from the 14th and 15th centuries. The fort dates from at least 1680 and its Martello tower was added in 1804. Batteries and barracks were added in the 19th century and during the German Occupation concrete bunkers were incorporated into the structure. These formed a strongpoint called 'Rotenstein'.

Walkers follow a path flanked by trees and bushes between fields and a golf course near Vazon

The granite headland features startling rocky outcrops and pinnacles. When the path swings round the end of the point to return to the coastal road, it is possible to appreciate how narrow the headland is. A few gnarled pines are passed as well as the site of the **Albecq** medieval settlement.

The path joins the main road at the head of a bay

and the road continues along the coast. A couple of small rocky points are rich in flowers and have little paths that allow them to be explored. When the road reaches Cobo Bay there are German bunkers flanking a slipway, and the Cobo Kiosk offers food and drink, with toilets and a bus stop nearby. ◄

To continue walking round the coast of Guernsey, walk through Cobo and refer to Walk 11.

A footpath across the road from the Cobo Kiosk is marked and signposted for Le Guet, up a flight of steps. Climb straight up a slope of pines to reach the **Rocque du Guet**. A bare point of granite pokes through this fortified site, and from a battery platform there is a remarkable view around Cobo Bay from Fort Hommet to the Grande Rocque Battery.

Army cadets form a military presence at the Rocque du Guet Watch House and Battery

Rocque du Guet Watch House and Battery was mentioned in 1581 and, on a part of Guernsey's coast where big cliffs are absent, it is certain that some form of watch was maintained from the Rocque du Guet at least as early as the 16th century. It was developed in its current form in the 18th century, and during the German Occupation the site was incorporated into the German coastal defence system.

Walk inland through the forest and follow a road out into the open to pass **St Matthew's Church**. A road junction is reached near a tall, curved stone wall. Turn right at this point and follow a narrow path, enclosed by bushes at first then running alongside a field to reach a road. Turn right down the road, **Rue du Tertre**, then turn left at a crossroads to follow a road called Les Quérités. Turn right down Rue de la Hougue, which itself turns left at Le Camp. Climb past La Hougue Batteries, which were built in 1796, before descending again. Follow the road to a junction with a busy road beside Belvoir House.

Cross the busy road and continue along a narrow road, La Bissonerie, past a cottage. A path runs onwards, enclosed by trees, bushes or tall walls. Turn right at the end to follow another busy road, Rue de la Porte, to **King's Mills**. Turn left along Rue à l'Eau, passing the King's Mills Water Treatment Works. Turn right up a narrower road, a *ruette tranquille*, called La Sauvarinerie, passing La Maison de Haut, and noticing the old washhouse opposite. Turn left a little way beyond the house to follow a wooded track uphill. This is concrete at first, then gravel, emerging from the trees with fine views over Vazon Bay.

When a road is reached, turn right to follow it downhill. Go straight through a crossroads where all four roads have high banks. Continue down the leafy Rue du Douit, another ruette tranquille, passing derelict glasshouses that once featured a Tomato Museum. Turn right to follow a main road alongside a large field, turning left down a narrow road alongside the same field. Keep straight onwards, following a narrow hedged track between more fields. There are flowery banks and flowery meadows, especially to the right. Later, there is a golf course on both sides of the track. A sandy track leads up to the main coastal road, where **La Grande Mare Hotel** stands to the right.

WALK 11

Cobo Bay and Saumarez Park

Distance	10km (6¼ miles)
Terrain	Easy coastal walking, with roads and paths followed further inland, exploring a well-wooded park and nature trail.
Start/Finish	Cobo Kiosk, Cobo
Refreshments	Plenty of choice around Cobo. Cafés available at Grandes Rocques, Port Soif and Saumarez Park.
Transport	Bus 2 links Cobo and Saumarez Park. Buses 3 and 3A serve the coast between Cobo and Port Soif, as well as Saumarez Park. Buses 7 and 7A also serve the coast road.

Cobo Bay offers easy coastal walking, followed by more easy walks around low, flowery points to reach Port Soif. A short walk inland leads to Saumarez Park, one of the few large parks on Guernsey. The grounds are quite well wooded and feature an interesting Folk Museum run by the National Trust of Guernsey. A pleasant wooded nature trail can be followed back to Cobo Bay to complete a circuit. For those with a bit more time and energy to spare, paths allow the route to be extended onto the fine viewpoint of Le Guet.

Start at the Cobo Kiosk and toilets on the south side of **Cobo Bay**. A slipway to the sandy beach is flanked by German bunkers. Either walk along the sandy beach while the tide is out, or along the main coastal road, past the village of **Cobo**. The Rockmount and Cobo Bay Hotels are available, as well as shops. ◄ At the next slipway, a path can be used between the main road and the beach, though one part is actually a linear car park. Opposite the Wayside Cheer Hotel, the path runs along a bank of spiky marram grass to reach a kiosk, toilets and small car park at **Grandes Rocques**.

Walkers on the beach can approach the village using a slipway.

The main road cuts straight through to Port Soif, but walkers can follow a fine easy path around a headland. The path passes the **Grandes Rocques Battery**, and there is also a solitary magazine building nearby. Keep left

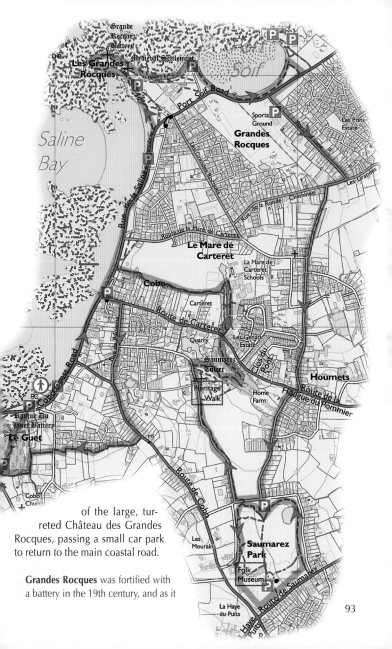

of the large, turreted Château des Grandes Rocques, passing a small car park to return to the main coastal road.

Grandes Rocques was fortified with a battery in the 19th century, and as it

The aptly-named Grandes Rocques rise from the end of a headland bearing a battery

was on a narrow headland, its line of fire could cover the bays to the north and south. The fortifications were further consolidated during the German Occupation, renaming the resultant strongpoint 'Grossfels'. The nearby Château des Grandes Rocques is impressive, constructed in baronial style. It was built to serve as a school for the Saumarez family in 1898 but has been converted into holiday apartments.

To continue walking round the coast of Guernsey, walk past the tea garden and refer to Walk 12.

Follow a path on a vegetated bank beside the road, above the bay of **Port Soif**. The beach is a remarkable little sandy crescent, while at low tide a rocky platform is exposed. Walkers could head for the Port Soif tea garden and toilets on the next point, but this walk runs inland by turning right along the next path to the main coastal road. ◄ The path running inland crosses the main road and turns right to reach **Port Soif Lane**. Turn left to follow the lane further inland, away from a sports ground. A notice indicates the circular Port Soif nature trail, which goes round the perimeter of the sports ground, exploring a fringe of tangled vegetation and a small pool. At the end of the road turn right, then left at **Grandes Mielles**, to follow Rue à Ronces. Keep left at the end to follow the busier Route de la Hougue du Pommier. This road passes entrances for the Guernsey Indoor Bowls Stadium, Indoor Cricket Guernsey and the Hotel Hougue du Pommier. Turn right at the top, then turn immediately left uphill along Rue des Houmets, a *ruette tranquille*. At the top of this road turn right and left to enter **Saumarez Park**.

SAUMAREZ PARK

The park has been developed since 1938, to preserve the house and grounds that once belonged to the Saumarez family. Parts of the former estate retain their original layout, but other features have been added. Of particular note is the Guernsey Folk and Costume Museum, managed by the National Trust of Guernsey, which has an entry charge, tel. 01481 255384, www.nationaltrust-gsy.org.gg. There is a series of buildings around a courtyard. Carefully arranged rooms display ordinary life in houses and farms over the past century. Kitchen, parlour, nursery and schoolroom can be studied, while a costume room displays items of clothing that are continually rotated. Farming and agricultural exhibits are housed in the other buildings. Apple presses are often found in the countryside, and the Cider Barn contains a reconstructed press. The National Trust of Guernsey also runs a small shop on site. Nearby is a restaurant, while the house formerly inhabited by the Saumarez family is now the Hostel of St John, a home for the elderly.

There is a perimeter path around the park, roughly square in plan. An

anti-clockwise circuit reveals the Guernsey Folk and Costume Museum first, followed by toilets, restaurant and the Hostel of St John. As the path continues around the park it passes a fine rose garden, a children's play area and a duckpond. Most of the perimeter is well wooded, but the central parts are grassy.

Leave the park by the same gateway that was used to enter it. Across the road from Saumarez Park is another gateway, signposted as the Saumarez Nature Trail. Follow a fine pathway, flanked by flowers, bushes and trees. There is a road just to the left, with a couple of exits onto it, but stay on the path throughout. When the path drifts away from the road and winds down a wooded slope into The Glen, it splits and later re-joins. Cross a busy road at a point where a disused footbridge is suspended between two stone towers. The path continues through a wooded area, and walkers should keep to the left of an overgrown old canal cutting, passing two footbridges. Later, drift left away from the old canal, following a wooded margin round the edge of playing fields near **Mare de Carteret School**. The path emerges into the open when it reaches the main coastal road at **Cobo Bay**.

The **Saumarez Nature Trail** is based on the path formerly used by the Saumarez family to reach the coast at Cobo. They had a footbridge built over a public road simply to avoid using the road. The trail is exceptionally well wooded, so walkers are hardly aware of nearby roads. The Ozanne Tower can be seen along the way, built as a folly and used for a while as a private museum. An overgrown ditch near a school was once a canal, constructed so that the Saumarez family could row their boats down to the sea.

A left turn leads straight into the village of **Cobo**, where the walk can be finished. However, it is worth continuing a little further to climb to a fine viewpoint. So, turn left inland past the shops at Cobo, then turn right at the NatWest bank to walk along Rue de Bouverie. Turn left at the end of the road along the busier Route de Cobo. Turn right along a narrow road marked as 'no through road', and follow it as it narrows further. A path continues round the back of some houses, reaching a minor road. Turn left and

immediately right to pick up another narrow path. At a junction, turn left, then right again, climbing up to a road called Ruette au Guet. Turn right again onto a pine-clad hill-top at **Le Guet**. A fine view around Cobo Bay is available from the Rocque du Guet Watch House and Battery. ▶ Walk steeply down a slope of pines, and down a flight of steps. Cross the main coastal road and turn right to return to the Cobo Kiosk.

A view of Cobo Bay at low water from the Rocque du Guet Watch House and Battery

See Walk 10 for details.

WALK 12
Portinfer and L'Islet

Distance	11km (7 miles)
Terrain	Easy coastal walking. Busy and quiet roads are followed inland.
Start/Finish	Port Soif
Refreshments	Cafés available at Port Soif, Rousse, L'Islet and Oatlands.
Transport	Buses 7 and 7A serve the coast between Port Soif and Le Grand Havre. Buses 5 and 5A (north), as well as 8 and 8A, run close to Guernsey Freesia Centre, Oatlands, Guernsey Candles and Pleinheaume.

Four fine little headlands and five bays can be enjoyed between Port Soif and Le Grand Havre. Despite the proximity of the main coastal road, there are plenty of coastal paths and a good footpath/cycleway beside the road. The walk moves inland to take in a number of attractions, including the Guernsey Freesia Centre, a craft village at Oatlands and Guernsey Candles. One stretch involves walking along a very busy main road, but a *ruette tranquille* is used afterwards and a remarkable meadow is passed.

If shooting is taking place, use an access road from a car park to by-pass the headland.

There is a deep active quarry just inland at Les Vardes, which might easily be passed unnoticed.

Start at **Port Soif**, where there is a café and toilets. A low-level coastal path drifts away from the road, flanked by grassy and flowery areas on a little headland, with a bouldery or pebbly beach alongside. A good path encircles the next bay at **Portinfer** then heads onto a point used by the Guernsey Clay Pigeon Shooting Club. ◄ The coastal path turns round the headland and joins a narrow road leading back to the main coastal road. A path accompanies the coastal road around the pebbly, bouldery **Baie des Pêqueries**. A hook-shaped headland at **Pulias** ends in a fine upstanding outcrop of rock, then a path continues round Baie de Pulias, passing the little pool of Pulias Pond.

◄ Follow the main coastal road for a while around Baie de Port Grat, passing a slipway and picking up another fine coastal path flanked by flowers. Looking ahead, Rousse Tower is a prominent feature that is worth some moments of careful study.

> The loopholed **Rousse Tower** was built in 1778, replacing a coastal battery. A new battery and magazine were added by 1804, with cannons pointing out to sea. When the tower is open the interior can be inspected free of charge. Life-sized models show how members of the Guernsey Militia and their families would have manned the defences. The magazine nearby contains further information and displays.

Rousse Tower overlooks Le Grande Havre and contains information about how it operated

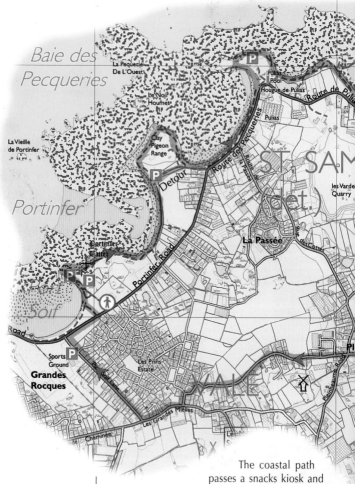

The coastal path passes a snacks kiosk and toilets, continuing through a small boatyard. Follow the path around Le Grande Havre, passing the Peninsula Hotel and Houmet Tavern. The path runs parallel to the coastal road, passing **Picquerel Point**, where a German bunker is embedded in a little headland. Flowers

grow thickly around the bay, while the path leads to a snacks kiosk near Vale Parish Church. ▶

To continue walking round the coast of Guernsey, walk past the snacks kiosk and refer to Walk 13.

Colin McCathie Nature Reserve is just across the main road from the snacks kiosk, through an archway in a stone wall that leads straight into a hide overlooking the reedy pool of **Vale Pond**. A variety of waders, ducks, geese and gulls all use the pool.

Double back along the main road and head inland from a junction along a road called Sandy Hook. The road overlooks Vale Pond and its surrounding wetlands. Pass a shop at **L'Islet** then turn left at the end of the road. Follow a straight road, Route Carre, further inland. The Guernsey Freesia Centre stands just to the left.

> **Guernsey Freesia Centre** occupies a three-acre site with an extensive area of glasshouses featuring a computerised growing environment. One large glasshouse might have 250,000 corms planted inside, which will produce around a million stems. Corms are planted throughout the year to ensure a constant supply of flowers for shipment. It has been calculated that eight out of ten freesias sold in the United Kingdom are grown on Guernsey. Roses and carnations are also popular. The Freesia Centre runs a video about Guernsey and the flower industry, while a shop on site offers a mail-order service for flowers. Tel. 01481 248185, **www.fletchers-freesias.co.uk**.

At the end of the road there are traffic lights controlling a very busy road junction. Cross straight through the junction and follow a path that veers left, passing Oatlands Nursery on the way to **Oatlands**.

> **Oatlands** comprises a number of old farm buildings around a courtyard, with two old brick kilns alongside. Notices explain about the interesting history of the site, with reference to other places around Guernsey. There are gift shops, a model shop, a dolls' house museum and a brasserie. Oatlands is open daily and entry is free, though there is a charge for some of the attractions, which include miniature golf and a go-kart track. Tel. 01481 241422.

Old brick-making kilns and plenty of other interesting features can be seen at Oatlands

Follow the path from **Oatlands** back to the busy junction and traffic lights. Turn left to follow the busy road that eventually passes the Guernsey Candles workshop. ▶ The workshop allows all the stages of the candle-making process to be observed. Multi-coloured layers of wax are added to candles, which are then cut and folded back to create the most amazingly colourful products.

Follow the busy road onwards, passing another set of traffic lights. The road bends left, and at this point it is possible to leave it by turning right along the quiet Rue à Chiens at **Les Annevilles**. The road turns left round a

Walkers who prefer not to follow this road may catch a bus.

103

A notice indicates the circular Port Soif nature trail, which goes round the perimeter of the sports ground, exploring a fringe of tangled vegetation and a small pool.

corner, then right at a junction, where it becomes a *ruette tranquille*. Follow it down past St Sampson Parochial Cemetery and later continue straight along Rue de la Cache. Walk uphill and turn left at a junction to reach a busy road at **Pleinheaume**. Cross the road and walk down Barras Lane, past a garage and houses. The road levels out and a huge meadow full of buttercups lies to the right. Later, there are houses on both sides and the road becomes very bendy. Two roads off to the right are dead-ends, but turn right at the next two junctions to follow **Port Soif Lane** straight back towards the coast at **Port Soif**. ◄

An enormous flowery meadow stretches into the distance when seen from Barras Lane

WALK 13

L'Ancresse and Vale

Distance	12km (7½ miles)
Terrain	Easy coastal paths round headlands and bays, returning inland on roads, tracks and paths.
Start/Finish	Vale Parish Church
Refreshments	Cafés and kiosks around Le Grande Havre and at L'Ancresse Bay. Pub and restaurant at L'Ancresse Bay, and a restaurant at the Beaucette Marina.
Transport	Buses 6 and 6A (north) run round the northern end of Guernsey, as well as 7 and 7A in the summer.

The route includes all the headlands and bays on the north coast. It then runs coast to coast along roads, tracks and paths to return to Vale Parish Church, which is one of the oldest churches on Guernsey.

CLOS DU VALLE

Until 1806 this walk would have been round the coast of an island completely separated from the rest of Guernsey by a tidal channel called Braye du Valle. The former island of Clos du Valle was susceptible to invasion; of the 15 stout loopholed towers built around the coast of Guernsey, nine were built round Clos du Valle, of which six remain standing. The tidal channel was drained during 1806–8; the resulting new land was sold and the money raised was used to construct two military roads. The only remnants of the channel are the inlet of St Sampson's harbour and the reedy Vale Pond, now a nature reserve below Vale Parish Church.

Start near Vale Parish Church at a snacks kiosk and car park at the head of **Le Grand Havre**. Follow a path round the eastern side of the bay, which is flanked by gorse and tall flowers. ▶ A car park, snack van and toilets are reached next to a children's play area. The path continues beside a golf course, though a sandy beach is available at low tide too. A kiosk and toilets appear towards the end of the bay, with tea gardens beyond a car park.

A variety of gulls and waders can often be seen round the bay.

La Benette

L'A
Bay

Fort
Pembroke

Star
Fort
Martello Tower No.9

Chouet

Mont
Cuet

Land
Fill
Site

Pembroke
Bay

Martello
Tower
No.10

Martello
Tower
No.7

La Varde
Dolmen

Hougues
Vanneaux

Ladies
Bay

Hommet
de Grève

Grand
Havre

Baie Des
Grèves

Les Clotures Road

Le Platte Mare Dolmen

Les
Fouaillages

Vale
Marais

Le Marais

La Grève

Amarreurs
Harbour

Le Hurel

La Garenne

Cemy

Les
Hougues
Pères

Ville
Baudu

La Ville Baudu

Pont St.
Michel

L'Abbaye

Vale
Pond

The coastal
path continues past
a loopholed tower and
magazine, and around the
next headland a small quarry

106

is used as an
oil dump. A large quarry at **Mont Cuet** is
used as a major landfill site, which can be smelly and
ugly. ▶ There used to be a huge German observation
tower on top of the hill, but it toppled headlong into the
quarry in 1991. Look out for an RSPB Marine Wildlife
Observatory in a bunker.

This can be avoided
by cutting inland
by road, but the
coast path round
the headland is both
attractively rocky and
flowery.

107

Looking along the beach at Baie de la Jaonneuse to a headland bearing Fort Pembroke

The sandy beach could be followed at low tide instead of the coastal path.

The loopholed tower at Baie de la Jaonneuse leans noticeably to one side, and one wonders what its ultimate fate will be! There is a small fortification on the end of the next narrow headland called **Fort Pembroke**, though some people take a short-cut and miss visiting it. Follow a path around **L'Ancresse Bay** (also known as Pembroke Bay), walking beside a concrete sea wall, passing a snacks kiosk and the Beach House restaurant. The latter has a rooftop viewing gallery and toilets. Pass close to two loopholed towers which stand beside the golf course on **L'Ancresse Common**. ◄ The sea wall ends at another kiosk and toilets, where the coastal path continues onto a well-fortified headland featuring two loopholed towers and **Fort le Marchant**. There is a firing range on the headland, and if red flags are flying and shooting is taking place, you will not be allowed beyond the first loopholed tower. Instead, follow a route clearly marked inland along a road and path to reach the next bay.

A path runs behind a series of high, cobbly storm beaches, leading to little **Fort Doyle** on a rocky headland beside a white house. Follow a path inland to pass behind the **Beaucette Marina**, which is in a flooded quarry where dark diorite bedrock is evident. ▶ Walk round the far side of the marina and keep well to the right of a boatyard to find a grassy path leading to a pebbly beach. Turn right and stay on top of a pebbly ridge, then follow a narrow path through low gorse scrub. A broader grassy path leads to a road bend at La Miellette. A tiny green islet sits out to sea, or is marooned amid bare rock at low tide.

A restaurant overlooks the boats moored in the water.

Follow a rather bendy road inland and uphill, passing houses and greenhouses. Keep right at a junction and walk a few paces up King's Road to visit **Le Déhus Dolmen**, which is just to the left of the road and in a fine state of preservation. Walk back along the King's Road afterwards to reach a junction with a busy main road. ▶

To continue walking round the coast of Guernsey, turn left and refer to Walk 14.

The complex passage grave of **Le Déhus Dolmen** dates from 3500BC. It has the usual mound, kerbstones, narrow entrance and broad chamber, with additional side chambers. The site was in danger of being demolished by quarrymen in 1775, but it was purchased to ensure its preservation. One huge capstone bears a unique carving, observed by switching on a specially angled light. This carving, unnoticed until 1916, depicts a bearded man holding a bow and arrows. The stone may once have been a single upright, before being reused as a capstone. The figure is now known as *Le Gardien du Tombeau*.

A signpost points right along the main road for L'Ancresse, but turn left down the main road first, then right along a quieter road called Petit Marais, signposted for Les Landes. This road is quite built-up, flanked by houses old and new, as well as greenhouses, some of which are in a derelict state. The Marais Reservoir lies to the left, in a flooded quarry, but is unseen. After passing a garage, walk through a crossroads at **Les Landes** and continue straight along a busier road. Turn right at a junction marked by a post box and green lamp-post. Follow the road, a *ruette tranquille*, until there is a sudden left turn, but keep straight on as marked 'no through road'. At the end of this road a footpath lies to the left, winding alongside walls for a while. When it reaches a road junction, walk straight onwards along La Vielle Marais. A huddle of old stone farm buildings gives way to newer buildings.

At a sharp right bend, a footpath squeezes beside a house called Le Chardronnet and runs between fields. Cross a road at **Le Hurel** and follow the continuation of the path. A narrow strip of tarmac runs beside a small stream, leading to a busy road facing onto a broad, triangular, grassy common. Turn left, then cross the road to walk up to **Vale Parish Church**. A path drops to the main road and returns to the snacks kiosk at the start.

The Ancient Priory and Parish Church of St Michel du Valle, or Vale Church for short

The hilltop site on which the **Ancient Priory and Parish Church of St Michel du Valle** stands obviously has a long

history as a religious site. The remains of a Neolithic burial chamber sit on top of the hill and the church lies just off the summit. A Benedictine Priory was founded around the year 968, though the foundation of the present church dates from the 12th century. Of particular note is the mixture of Norman and Romanesque features, and the rather large piscina near the altar. The churchyard is full of gravestones and the cemetery area has been considerably extended. Many of the stones prove to be quite interesting and it is worth wandering around to spot some of the more unusual ones.

WALK 14
St Sampson and Belle Grève Bay

Distance	10km (6¼ miles)
Terrain	Busy and quiet roads, with short coastal paths and a small park.
Start	The Bridge, St Sampson
Finish	Liberation Monument, St Peter Port
Refreshments	Plenty of choice around St Sampson and St Peter Port.
Transport	Buses 6 and 6A (north) and 7 and 7A serve St Sampson. All bus services on Guernsey converge on St Peter Port.

St Sampson lies in an interesting part of Guernsey where the landscape has changed significantly over the past two centuries. The harbour was developed from a channel, Braye du Valle, which once separated Guernsey from the smaller island of Clos du Valle. A short circular walk from town takes in the nearby countryside and coast, returning through an industrial area. The route leaves town again via Delancey Park. A simple coastal walk round the built-up Belle Grève Bay leads to the harbour in St Peter Port.

'The Bridge' at **St Sampson** dates only from 1806, built after the tidal channel of Braye du Valle was drained. The harbour was constructed in its present form soon afterwards. After the conclusion of the Napoleonic Wars in 1815 shipyards were opened around St Sampson. One of the most notable features on the harbourside is Le Crocq Clock Tower. This was built in 1873 and has served as the Harbourmaster's Office and lock-up. The harbour is mostly used for the import of oil and gas to generate power for Guernsey.

Start on **The Bridge** in St Sampson and follow the main road northwards, signposted for L'Ancresse. Go straight through a crossroads, following Route des Coutures onwards. The road is walled and overhung with trees as it climbs gently uphill. Go straight through another crossroads, passing **Vale Infant School**. The road turns

111

The old windmill tower of Vale Mill was extended skywards during the German Occupation

Le Déhus Dolmen is just a short walk up King's Road. This diversion is well worth the few minutes it takes, retracing your steps afterwards. See Walk 13.

right, but continue where marked 'no entry', passing another entrance to the school. The road turns left, then right, among houses. Turn right at a junction, and a short way up the road, turn left to continue climbing to Vale Mill Cottages. The tower of Vale Mill is a prominent landmark in this area.

Vale Mill windmill was constructed in 1850 and has been a prominent landmark ever since. Its sails have long since vanished, but the stout tower was extended skywards during the German Occupation to form an observation tower. The mill tower is now a dwelling house and must provide a most impressive view.

Follow the road straight downhill, passing the Methodist Church at Bordeaux and turning left along a main road at the bottom. Follow the road until it turns left, but at that point turn right along Les Croutes. ◀ Continue to a crossroads at **La Turquie**, where a road runs straight to the sea and a rocky shore, with a small, grassy island offshore.

Turn right to follow a coastal track and path, or climb a few steps to follow a maze of paths between trees and clumps of gorse at a higher level. There is a car park on a point and a couple of grassy islets lie offshore at **Hommet**. A path runs between a road and the coast, then a short stretch of road has to be followed. A car park, toilets and a kiosk are passed

on a broad, grassy area. There are two
paths available – one on the left of the
road, passing through bushes close
to the coast, the other running
to the right of

Map continues on
page 114

113

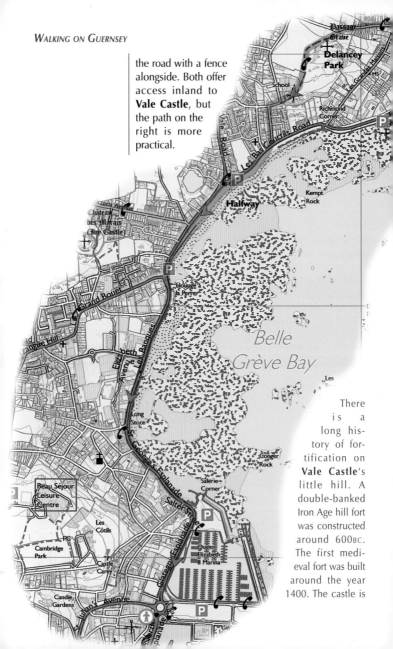

the road with a fence alongside. Both offer access inland to **Vale Castle**, but the path on the right is more practical.

There is a long history of fortification on **Vale Castle**'s little hill. A double-banked Iron Age hill fort was constructed around 600BC. The first medieval fort was built around the year 1400. The castle is mentioned in the 16th and 17th centuries, but only assumed its current shape in the 18th century. Extensive barrack-building took place and paved roads ran between the buildings. These can still be seen although the barracks have been demolished. This was the main fortification for defending Clos du Valle when it was, until 1806, a separate island lying north of Guernsey. The castle was again strengthened during the German Occupation.

After looking round the castle and enjoying views from its curtain walls, walk down to the main road and follow it alongside the industrial harbour back to **The Bridge** in St Sampson. Walk round the south side of the harbour, passing the clock tower at Le Crocq, then turn right up Church Street to reach St Saviour's Church. This stands next to an old quarry which has been flooded to form the Longue Hougue Reservoir.

Cranes beside the industrial harbour on the way back into St Sampson

The present **St Sampson's Parish Church** dates from the 12th century and was built over a long period, nearing completion around 1350, which accounts for the rather rugged look of its masonry. St Sampson, the patron saint of Guernsey, landed on the island some time before 550BC. He was a missionary from Dol in Brittany, and may have founded a church where the parish church now stands. St Magloire, who was a cousin of St Sampson, also has a place in the Christian history of the Channel Islands. He is associated with an early settlement on the island of Sark.

Keep following Church Street and continue straight along a main road. Turn right up a minor road called Mont Morin. At the top, on the left, is an entrance to **Delancey Park**. Follow a tarmac path all the way through this grassy and partly-wooded space, with good views of the coast from the top. Walk down from the park, along Rue du Monts, turning left to follow Delancey Lane to the busy coastal road.

Turn right to follow the coast round **Belle Grève Bay**, walking along a broad and grassy strip between the road and the sea, past La Tonnelle. At the Red Lion there is a path beside the sea wall, while a bunker built into the wall is planted with flowers and makes a pleasant viewpoint. ◄ Stretches of sandy beach may be followed at low tide, but some parts are pebbly or rocky. Large modern buildings of polished stone and glass are passed, as well as a slipway at **Longstore**. Older rows of houses include occasional pubs, restaurants, cafés and shops.

Pass a little harbour at the end of **St George's Esplanade** and turn round a corner to follow Glategny Esplanade. A large car park projects seawards and a large **marina** appears alongside, and the walk is practically over. The Liberation Monument at the Weighbridge makes a good place to end and all the facilities of St Peter Port are immediately to hand.

There was a loopholed tower nearby, one of 15 that once stood around the coast, but it has been demolished.

Looking back around Belle Grève Bay to the wooded slopes of Delancey Park

WALK 15

Beau Sejour and Le Friquet

Distance	9km (5½ miles)
Terrain	Mostly road walking, with a couple of short tracks and parkland paths.
Start/Finish	Beau Sejour Centre, St Peter Port
Refreshments	Cafés at Beau Sejour, Island Bowl and Le Friquet. A pub is available on the way back into St Peter Port.
Transport	Buses 1, 1A, 2, 5 and 5A (north) serve different parts of the route, but all parts are within easy walking distance of St Peter Port.

So you like to walk? Others like to play football, rugby, cricket, or race go-karts. Some just like to potter in their gardens, while children are happy to run round the park. This walk wanders through the suburbs and countryside near St Peter Port, passing several sport and leisure venues. The intensity of land use and the wealth of building styles are also remarkable. Bear in mind that most parts of this walk are built up and some roads are busy. Tucked away in all sorts of unlikely places are interesting heritage features waiting to be discovered.

The grounds of **Cambridge Park** are planted with a variety of mature trees. A simple stroll can be enjoyed while other people are engaged in more energetic pursuits.

The **Beau Sejour Centre** caters for all sorts of pastimes, indoor and outdoor sports and health and fitness activities, catering for children and adults as well as hosting cultural events. Holiday membership is available, tel. 01481 747222, **www.freedomzone.gg**.

The Beau Sejour Centre in **Cambridge Park** is easily reached on foot from any part of St Peter Port, or it can be reached by bus. Start at the entrance to the centre on Amherst Road and walk down a road marked as 'no entry'. Continue through a crossroads from Amherst Road

117

onto Mont Arrivé. At the bottom of the road continue straight along **Grand Bouet**. Turn left along a road signposted for Château des Marais, walking off the end of the road to reach castle ruins lost among trees.

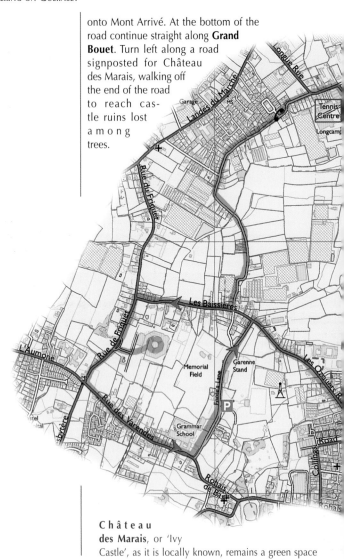

Château des Marais, or 'Ivy Castle', as it is locally known, remains a green space

St Sampson's
Marais

Hougue
Nicolle

Track

Rabbit
Warren

Victoria Avenue
Chateau
des Marais
(Ivy Castle)

Hougue des
Cartiers

Les
Quartiers

Ramée

Coutanchez

Route des Coutanchez

Pitronnerie
Rd Ind Est

Grand Bouet

Pitronnerie Road

La Vrangue Hill

La Vrangue

de la Ramée

Post
Office

Mont Arrivé

La Couture

School

Amherst Road

Beau Séjour
Leisure
Centre

Rozel Road

St Jacques

Cambridge
Park

La Butte

Lane

Les
Rocquettes

Mont Grove

St PETER
PORT

Candie Road

Victoria
Tower

De

School

Doyle R

119

Château des Marais, or Ivy Castle, is almost lost among trees and bushes outside St Peter Port

A range of plants are grown for sale at GROW.

Carved as 'St Pierre Port i Le Valle'.

among the urban sprawl. The rocky mound is known to have been used in the Bronze Age, when it stood above an area of marshland. The visible fortifications date from the early 13th century, when the mound was encircled by a moat, an earth bank and a stone wall. For additional security an outer wall was added. The whole site was strengthened and largely rebuilt in the 18th century, when a magazine was also constructed on the mound. A concrete bunker was added during the German Occupation.

Leave the mound and walk through the grassy space between the moat and the outer wall to find the only other breach, where a short path leads to a new housing development and **Victoria Avenue**. Turn left to follow the avenue towards two large buildings, The Island Bowl to the left and a football pitch and go-kart track to the right. Walk between these and the road becomes a track enclosed first by walls, then by bushes and brambles. Follow the track and it later becomes a narrow road passing several small houses at the Bukit Estate. Turn left to reach a crossroads and go straight ahead along the Verte Rue, passing the Guernsey Rural Occupation Workshop (GROW). ◄

Keep straight ahead at a junction, walking past greenhouses full of flowers. Turn right at a junction to follow the busy **Route des Longs Camps**. This later turns left, but when it turns right afterwards, walk straight ahead along the quieter Pont Vaillant. Follow this bendy road onwards, avoiding all other junctions. There are plenty of houses at first, followed by an open stretch where a stone over a stream marks the boundary between the parishes of St Peter Port and Vale. ◄ Turn right along another busy road, **Les Baissières**, passing Baissière Farm. Here, a stone over a stream marks the junction of the parishes

Château des Marais, or Ivy Castle, is almost lost among trees and bushes outside St Peter Port

A range of plants are grown for sale at GROW.

Carved as 'St Pierre Port i Le Valle'.

among the urban sprawl. The rocky mound is known to have been used in the Bronze Age, when it stood above an area of marshland. The visible fortifications date from the early 13th century, when the mound was encircled by a moat, an earth bank and a stone wall. For additional security an outer wall was added. The whole site was strengthened and largely rebuilt in the 18th century, when a magazine was also constructed on the mound. A concrete bunker was added during the German Occupation.

Leave the mound and walk through the grassy space between the moat and the outer wall to find the only other breach, where a short path leads to a new housing development and **Victoria Avenue**. Turn left to follow the avenue towards two large buildings, The Island Bowl to the left and a football pitch and go-kart track to the right. Walk between these and the road becomes a track enclosed first by walls, then by bushes and brambles. Follow the track and it later becomes a narrow road passing several small houses at the Bukit Estate. Turn left to reach a crossroads and go straight ahead along the Verte Rue, passing the Guernsey Rural Occupation Workshop (GROW). ◄

Keep straight ahead at a junction, walking past greenhouses full of flowers. Turn right at a junction to follow the busy **Route des Longs Camps**. This later turns left, but when it turns right afterwards, walk straight ahead along the quieter Pont Vaillant. Follow this bendy road onwards, avoiding all other junctions. There are plenty of houses at first, followed by an open stretch where a stone over a stream marks the boundary between the parishes of St Peter Port and Vale. ◄ Turn right along another busy road, **Les Baissières**, passing Baissière Farm. Here, a stone over a stream marks the junction of the parishes of Vale, St Peter Port, St Andrew and Castel. ▶ There is a shop at the end of the road, and a left turn along the busy **Rue du Friquet** leads to Le Friquet.

Carved as 'Le Valle, St Pierre Port, St André, Le Castel'.

LE FRIQUET HOME OF GARDEN AND LIVING

Le Friquet has been many things over the years. It was once the Guernsey Flower and Butterfly Centre, becoming Le Friquet Centre of Attractions later. In 2009 an impressive garden centre opened, centred on an enormous octagonal building containing a circular walkway through the entire building. The site must offer the longest covered walk you could complete on Guernsey, and there is a café half-way round! The building also contains a lecture room and a programme of talks may be posted. The building encloses a large outdoor space filled by a fine expanse of shrubs and flowers, protected by a glass canopy shaped like the big top of a circus. The site is open daily and is free to visit. www.bluediamond.gg.

Leaving Le Friquet, continue along the busy road to reach traffic lights and turn left along **Rue des Varendes**. The road is quite built up and leads to another set of lights at Les Varendes, where a left turn leads down Foote's Lane. Walk past the **Grammar School** and Sixth Form Centre, passing a variety of sports grounds including football, rugby and cricket, a running track and other athletics facilities. At another set of traffic lights turn right to follow the road past St Peter Port Secondary School and Les Ouzets Lodge. Rise to a junction with the busy Collings Road and cross straight over to continue up a narrow road, Valnord Lane, overhung by holm oak and sycamore trees. Turn left at the top, noting the John Wesley Stone across the road.

John Wesley visited Guernsey twice during 1787, as well as Jersey and Alderney, and he stayed at the nearby house of Mon Plaisir as the guest of Henri de Jersey. He preached in the house, but when the congregation grew too large he preached outside. It is believed that this stone, an old riding mount, was where he stood to deliver his sermons. Wesley was well received in

John Wesley is said to have preached from a roadside mounting block above St Peter Port

the Channel Islands and a number of Methodist churches are evident while travelling around the islands.

Follow the road onwards, down through a staggered crossroads and down past the Taverne St Jacques. The road dips and rises, flanked by many fine old buildings, reaching the German Naval Signals Headquarters and a hotel at the top.

When they first occupied Guernsey, the Germans' **Naval Signals Headquarters** were based in La Collinette Hotel and La Porte Hotel. For greater security they built two concrete bunkers linked by a tunnel, operational from February 1944. The bunker housed powerful radio equipment which, after the effective isolation of the Channel Islands following the D-Day landings in Normandy in September 1944, provided the only link between the German forces on Guernsey and their commanders in Berlin. The bunker has been re-fitted based on information supplied by the original officer in charge, Willi Hagedorn. Opening times are limited: April to October, Thursday and Saturday, 1400–1700. There is an entrance charge, tel. 07781 107632, **www.occupied.guernsey.net**.

Continue along the road, straight ahead along Elm Grove, and turn left at the traffic lights to walk along La Butte. Look for an opening in the wall on the right to enter the grounds of **Cambridge Park**. A path runs inside the park, parallel to the road, quickly returning walkers to the Beau Sejour Centre.

WALK 16

St Martin and La Villette

Distance	5km (3 miles)
Terrain	Mostly road walking, with occasional tracks and paths.
Start/Finish	St Martin's Parish Church
Refreshments	A choice of places at St Martin's. There are also two hotel bars along the way.
Transport	Buses 5 and 5A (south), 6 and 6A (south), 7 and 7A serve St Martin's. 5 and 5A (south), 6 and 6A (south) run close to Catherine Best Jewellery.

People regularly visit St Martin's Parish Church to admire the curious statue–menhir of *La Gran'mère du Chimquière*. With an hour or two to spare, a short walk can be taken through nearby suburbs and countryside. A prominent 19th century windmill tower along the way houses the Catherine Best Jewellery workshop. There are old and new houses scattered around the fields, along with busy and quiet roads. Occasional short paths and tracks break up the road-walking.

St Martin's Parish Church is also known as St Martin de la Bellouse, standing beside the healing spring of La Fontaine de la Bellouse. An early church on this site, mentioned in 1048, may have been a wooden construction. The stone building dates from the 13th century and there have been additions to the structure through the centuries. A number of articles of antiquity are preserved, including an old baptismal font, pulpit and lectern.

The female statue–menhir of La Gran'mère du Chimquière stands at the entrance to St Martin's Parish Church

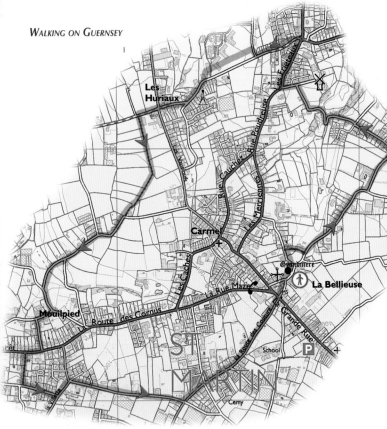

The statue–menhir of **La Gran'mère du Chimquière** stands at the gate of St Martin's churchyard. She is clearly a 'sister' of the statue–menhir at Castel Parish Church, seen on Walk 17. The stone dates from the Late Neolithic or Early Bronze Age, around 2500–1800BC, though has later embellishments, possibly from Roman times. The statue has been broken in two, and previously it stood closer to the church. Visitors often find the 'Gran'mère' wearing a garland of flowers, or with a few coins balanced on her head.

Start at **St Martin's** by visiting the 'Gran'mère' and the church. Leave the churchyard using a gate round the back. Turn left along a road and right down a lovely, short, grassy lane past a few old houses to reach La Douit Farm. Turn left up a road, Les Traudes, climbing gently past Ballieuse Farm and other buildings. Turn left at the Green Acres Hotel at Les Hubits, and left again at a crossroads, along La Rue du Varivaray. Pass a few houses and keep straight ahead through a cross-roads, following a narrow and bendy road down into a wooded valley and up the other side. A prominent **windmill tower** is seen to the right, where Catherine Best Jewellery may be visited; otherwise turn left to reach a busy road.

Turn right along the busy road to reach a garage with a shop at a crossroads. Turn left at the crossroads and follow the road called Oberlands, which passes the quiet side of the Princess Elizabeth Hospital. Use a path running parallel to the road, just inside the hospital grounds. Further along the road, keep right at a junction and walk straight through a crossroads to follow Rue des Huriaux

A path through the grounds of Princess Elizabeth Hospital allows a short break from road-walking

A large building on the left contains food and confectionery, which is delivered to outlets all over Guernsey, from hotels to beach cafés.

at **Les Huriaux**. ◄ Turn left along a grassy track passing between fields. Continue straight along a road, a *ruette tranquille* called La Planque, avoiding a turning to the right and another to the left. The road is flanked by flowers and trees. Turn left uphill at a 'T' junction, then right up to **Mouilpied** and its fine stone houses. Turn left up La Ruette de la Pompe to reach the busy main road of Route de la Forêt.

Turn right along the busy road to pass a large house, Château du Bois, then turn left at a bus stop to follow a tarmac path flanked by hedges, La Trelade Lane. Turn left along a narrow road until a 'T' junction is reached at **La Villette**. To the right is La Villette Hotel, but turn left to reach a crossroads at La Villette Garage. Turn right as signposted for the Moulin Huet Pottery. The narrow road, a ruette tranquille called La Rue des Escaliers, passes a playground and runs through a patchwork landscape of fields and greenhouses. Turn left at a crossroads, pass a row of houses at Rockwell Terrace, then walk straight through the next crossroad, following **Route des Coutures**. Pass St Martin's Primary School on the way back to the main road near **St Martin's Parish Church**.

La Rue des Escaliers at La Villette is a ruette tranquille heading back towards St Martin's

WALK 17

St Andrew and Castel

Distance	7km (4½ miles)
Terrain	Mostly road walking, but with some tracks and paths.
Start/Finish	St Andrew's Parish Church
Refreshments	Garage shop near Castel Church.
Transport	Buses 4, 5 and 5A (south) serve St Andrew's Church and the Little Chapel. 5 and 5A (south) also serve Castel Church.

Quiet roads can be followed around St Andrew and Castel, starting and finishing at St Andrew's Parish Church. The countryside is mostly filled with farms and fields, though plenty of houses have been built in some places. The two parish churches are quite old and interesting, and another feature of interest on the walk is the German Underground Hospital. While most of the walk is along roads, there are some good paths and tracks which can be used, particularly in the lovely, wooded Talbot Valley, where an old watermill is an added attraction.

St Andrew's Parish Church is also known as St Andre de la Pommeraye and lies couched in a wooded valley close to the healing spring of La Fontaine de St Clair. The walls supported a wooden roof, which was replaced with stone vaulting in the 13th century. Although the church appears to be quite small, it is in fact twice its original size.

Start near **St Andrew's Church**, following a road called La Vassalerie which is signposted for the German Underground Hospital. It is worth taking a break at this early stage to explore the site, which is the largest tunnel system in the Channel Islands.

Les Effards

Obelisk

Statue Menhir

MS

Rue du Preel

Route de l'Eglise

Le Preel

Les Touillets

Rue Piette

La Chaumière

Route des Talbots

Talbot Valley

Les Niaux

Les Galiennes

La Monnaie Chapel

Rue du Monnaie

Camptréhard

Les Poidevins

l'Écluse

Four Cabot

St Andrews Road

Candie Road

P

School

St Ar Resr.

Les Naftiau

GERMAN MILITARY UNDERGROUND HOSPITAL

This extensive tunnel system was an underground hospital and ammunition store. The hospital was in use for only a few weeks, after the D-Day landings in Normandy, while most of the ammunition was never used. Hundreds of slave workers under the German Organisation Todt hacked out the tunnels, which were lined with concrete and equipped with heating and air conditioning. The tunnels were gas-proof, with only two entrances and three escape shafts. There was also an enormous underground reservoir. While much has been removed, some original fittings and contents remain. The tunnels are cool and damp, and visitors guide themselves round by referring to numbered signs. At the entrance there are displays of Occupation memorabilia, including press cuttings from the war years, and supporting literature is on sale. There is an entrance charge, tel. 01481 239100. Hand in your ticket when you leave, so they know everyone is out before they turn off the lights in the evening!

Continue walking along La Vassalerie to reach a crossroads at **Les Naftiaux**. Turn left here, and almost immediately left again, to follow Rue de la Boullerie. Walk straight ahead, passing through a staggered crossroads beside a former chapel. Cross over a busy road and continue straight down a leafy, wooded track. Turn left at the bottom, right and right again along a road, then left to walk up **Rue du Monnaie** from a waterpump. Part way up the road is a left turn for Monnaie Chapel, or Les Galliennes Chapel, but this is signposted 'for private worship only', and is not for general visitors. Cross over another busy road at La Monnaie and continue along Rue des Truchots, heading downhill. Follow the narrow road past the GSPCA Animal Shelter and turn left at the bottom. The road climbs uphill and a left turn leads past **Castel Church**, which is worth visiting.

CASTEL PARISH CHURCH

The church is also known as Ste Marie du Castro, said to have been built on the site of an ancient castle. It was first mentioned in 1155, when it was a ▶

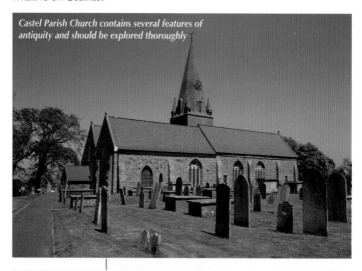

Castel Parish Church contains several features of antiquity and should be explored thoroughly

possession of Mont St Michel in France, and parts of the building date from the 11th and 12th centuries. Interesting frescoes on the walls date from the 13th century. Some indication of the age of the building can be gained by studying odd features in the exterior stonework, where doorways have been blocked and new windows opened.

A statue–menhir beside the door is clearly a 'sister' of the *Gran'mère du Chimquière* at St Martin's Parish Church. It dates from the Late Neolithic or Early Bronze Age, around 2500-1800BC, and shows signs of later embellishments. It was discovered in 1878 buried under the chancel of the church. A bell-casting pit was discovered at the same time, now covered by a glass plate in the floor of the church. Excavations in 1999 brought Roman remains to light, and other artefacts dating back 5000 years, now preserved in the church.

Follow the busy road, **Route de l'Église**, away from the crossroads beside Castel Church, passing a garage with a shop, and a fine grassy space called Fairfield. After passing a tall transmitter mast, turn left along a *ruette tranquille*, Rue des Morts, to pass a covered reservoir. Continue along a path marked as La Fourchure, which has flowery banks and hedgerows, passing fields and greenhouses as it runs down towards the Talbot Valley. Turn left along a road, then when the road turns left uphill, turn right down a narrow path. This steep and stony path drops down into the wooded lower parts of the **Talbot Valley**. Just as a road is reached, steps to the right allow access to the optional 'Ron Short Walk'.

Optional Extension – Ron Short Walk
This path was created by the National Trust of Guernsey, running out and back across a wooded slope. If this short circular walk is included in the route, then return to this point to continue. The extra distance is 1km (½ mile).

Follow the road gently up through the valley to continue, taking note of a flowery meadow to the right which is another National Trust of Guernsey property. Turn right along a narrow road marked **Les Niaux** to cross a little river, passing the Moulin des Niots (or Niaux), noting its overshot mill wheel. The narrow, bendy road climbs steeply, rising to gentler fields above.

When the highest part of the road is reached, turn left along another quiet road. There is a dip in this road later, where it passes a couple of houses. Climb uphill turning right and left at a staggered crossroads to follow La Rue des Morts. This is another bendy road, which finally drops between graveyards to return to **St Andrew's Church.**

A fine path between Castel and a series of National Trust for Guernsey properties in the Talbot Valley

WALK 18

King's Mills and Fauxquets

Distance	9km (5½ miles)
Terrain	Quiet *ruettes tranquilles*, woodland tracks and a narrow field path.
Start/Finish	King's Mills
Refreshments	Restaurants available near the airport and in the Fauxquets Valley.
Transport	Buses 5 and 5A (south) serve King's Mills and the Little Chapel. Bus 4 also serves the Little Chapel.

An interesting walk can be enjoyed from King's Mills, using a track to climb to a fine viewpoint. Quiet roads can be followed past farms and fields, passing close to Guernsey Airport. Not far away, in the lovely valley of Vauxbelets, is the celebrated Little Chapel. This amazing structure is constructed entirely of broken crockery and ceramic tiles. The wooded valleys of Vauxbelets and Fauxquets are followed back to King's Mills. Almost all the roads followed on this circuit are quiet ruettes tranquilles.

Leave **King's Mills** by following **Rue à l'Eau**, passing the King's Mills Water Treatment Works. Turn right up a narrower road, a ruette tranquille called La Sauvarinerie, passing La Maison de Haut, and notice the old wash-house opposite. Turn left a little way beyond the house to follow a wooded track uphill. This is concrete at first, then gravel, emerging from the trees with fine views over Vazon Bay.

When a road is reached, turn left up Rue de la Petite Hurette, then turn right to walk along Rue de la Haye, passing an old water trough. Keep straight on along the road, avoiding junctions to right and left, admiring some of the fine stone buildings along the way, as well as another old water trough along Rue des Caches. Cross over a main road and continue straight onwards from **Les Prevosts**, from one ruette tranquille to another. Keep left at three road junctions and right at the next, reaching a

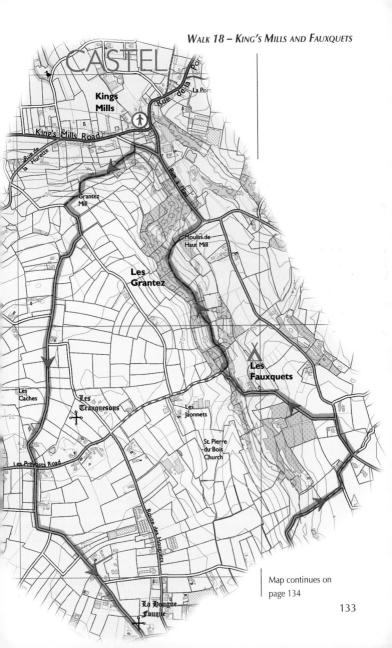

CASTEL

Kings Mills

La Port

Rue de la Por

King's Mills Road

Rue de la Hurette

Grantez Mill

Rue a Jean

Moulin de Haut Mill

Les Grantez

Les Fauxquets

Les Caches

Les Tranquesous

Les Jaonnets

St. Pierre du Bois Church

Les Prévosts Road

Route des Houards

La Hougue Fouque

Map continues on page 134

The Farmhouse Hotel and its restaurant lie to the right.	crossroads at a busy main road. ◀ Keep straight ahead and pass the Specsavers factory. Turn

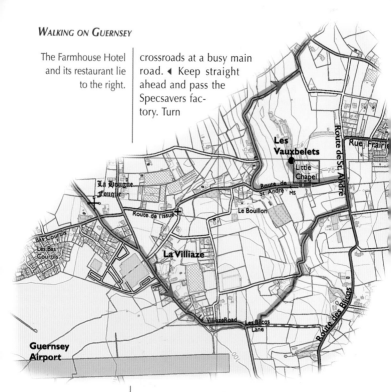

Map continues on page 133

right along a busier road, which later runs beside the securely-fenced **Guernsey Airport**.

When the road turns right around a corner of the airport fence, walk straight ahead down a narrow road, and turn left along a narrow path. The path is well-vegetated and would leave you drenched if the plants were wet. It runs down to a minor road, Ruette des Norgiots, which is followed further down and uphill. Turn left down Rue des Blicqs and left again down the busy Bouillon Road, then turn right along a narrow road signposted for the Little Chapel and Guernsey Clockmakers, which are worth a short detour at **Les Vauxbelets**.

Construction of the amazing **Little Chapel** started in 1923, the work being carried out by Brother Deodat

The Little Chapel is decorated throughout with broken pieces of decorated ceramic plates

and Brother Christian of the De La Salle Order. Masses of clinker were cemented together to form the shape of the chapel, then almost every surface was covered with bits of broken pottery, ceramics, mirrors, tiles, pebbles and shells. In an effort to create something similar to a structure at Lourdes in France, the edifice has been pulled down a couple of times in the quest for perfection. Wedgwood donated the ceramic pieces for the lower steps, and while admission is free, there is a request for donations.

The **Guernsey Clockmakers workshop** is a short way along the road from the Little Chapel. All manner of clocks are fashioned and sold, from traditional designs to rather bizarre modern timepieces.

A narrow but passable path drops from the airport towards the wooded head of the Fauxquets Valley

Walk back along the road from the Little Chapel and turn right, then right again. A ruette tranquille, Le Grais Lane, runs along the side of a grassy and flowery valley bearing a few clumps of trees. The road drops to cross a little river in a stone channel, then climbs steeply uphill. Turn left at a crossroads at the top, then left again along Rue des Fauxquets. The road drops from fields, past apple orchards, into the wooded **Les Fauxquets** Valley, where the Haybarn bar and restaurant is available.

Again, the little river which drains the valley can be seen in a stone channel where it goes under the road, and a stone marks the parish boundary between Castel and St Saviour. Follow the road uphill and turn right along a woodland track called Rue Paintain. This track is flanked with flowers and a variety of trees, running along a slope above the watery valley. ◀ The track runs down from the wood, crossing the valley and passing a few old stone houses at **Moulin de Haut**. Turn left along a busy road, **Rue à l'Eau** again, to return to **King's Mills**.

Woodpeckers and treecreepers can be observed in the woods, while sparrowhawks and barn owls hunt through the valley.

WALK 19

Rocquaine Bay and Quanteraine

Distance	6km (3¾ miles)
Terrain	Quiet roads, tracks and field paths.
Start/Finish	Rocquaine Bay
Refreshments	Café off-route near the start, at Guernsey Pearl.
Transport	Buses 5 and 5A (south) and 7 and 7A serve Roquaine Bay; 5 and 5A (south) also pass La Longue Roque.

This short walk heads inland from Rocquaine Bay. It wanders nowhere in particular, but takes advantage of short paths and tracks, linked with narrow roads to make a lovely quiet circuit. There is a nature reserve, a couple of wooded valleys, patchwork fields at a higher level, several fine stone buildings and the old Moulin de Quanteraine. This was the last watermill to operate on Guernsey and is now a National Trust of Guernsey property. Another feature of interest is the tall standing stone of La Longue Rocque.

Although this walk lies inland, it starts on the coast at **Rocquaine Bay**, at a road junction near the 'Wood Works' workshop, between Fort Grey and L'Erée. There is a large concrete bunker built into the sea wall, where a road runs inland from a triangular junction and post box. Follow the road inland and turn left along Rue des Vicheris, passing the Orchid Fields.

The **Bridget Ozanne Orchid Fields** are an amazing sight early in the summer. The four most common species seen are the common spotted, heath spotted, southern marsh and loose-flowered orchids. The fields are privately owned, but are leased to La Société Guernsiaise, **www.societe.org.gg**. Access is provided around some of the field margins to enable the orchids, and a multitude of other plants, to be seen more closely.

The Bridget Ozanne Orchid Fields abound in colour and interest throughout spring and early summer

Turn right at a crossroads along Rue de la Pomare, following the narrow road up past a few houses and the older **La Pomare Farm**. Turn left up a narrow road, which becomes a track rising past a water trough. Keep right at a junction, and the track has flowery banks and a few trees alongside. It winds uphill, and when a road is joined at the top, walk straight along it. Turn a left bend then turn right at a junction, reaching a main road at the end of Rue du Val.

Turn left along the main road, then right at La Pointe Farm, along Rue du Lorier. Follow the road downhill then turn right up a narrow path. This path has flowery banks and passes between fields, leading back to the main road. Cross over to see **La Longue Rocque** standing in a field.

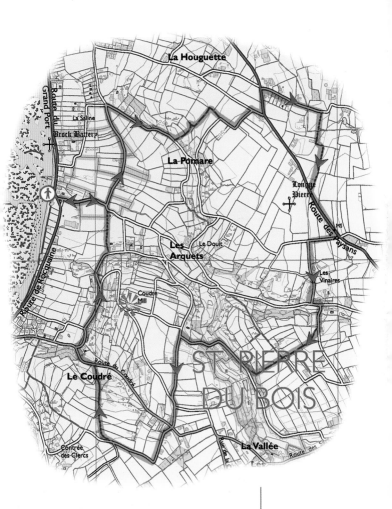

La Longue Rocque, or **Longue Pierre**, is the tallest menhir, or standing stone, on Guernsey. It rises 3.5m from
the ground and stands in complete isolation in a large
field, where cattle use it as a scratching post. Legend
says that it is a fairy cricket bat, brought up from the sea
and planted in the field!

La Longue Rocque is a standing stone put to good use as a scratching post by Guernsey cows!

Walk up the main road then turn right down a minor road. Turn left down another minor road, Rue des Juliennes, passing some fine old stone houses at **Les Vinaires**. Turn left and right to follow a narrow road called Rue des Grandes Rues up to a house called Le Val des Prés, which is on the left. Opposite the house, heading off to the right, is a narrow, flowery path, flanked by trees and bushes. It rises between fields to reach a road junction. Walk straight through the junction and down a narrow road and a sunken, well-wooded path with steps, into a valley. Turn right to follow a road down through the valley to Le Moulin de Quanteraine.

A statement about the history of **Le Moulin de Quanteraine**, a 16th century watermill, is posted beside the road. It is a National Trust of Guernsey property, though privately let and not available for visits, but it can be viewed from the road. It was the last watermill to operate on Guernsey, closing in the 1930s. The waterwheel survived into the 1940s and was restored in 1991. As well as grinding corn, the mill also powered a threshing machine in a nearby barn.

Follow the road up out of the valley, turning left at a junction to climb further uphill. Keep left, then right, at junctions on top and follow the road down to a crossroads. Go straight through the crossroads, climb uphill and turn right. There are fine views extending around Rocquaine Bay and L'Erée Bay. Fork right to follow a track downhill and views continue to be good until they are blocked by high banks, bushes and trees further down. Turn left down a main road at **Le Coudré**, then right along a minor road. Keep right at the next junction, climbing gently, then left down a narrow road. Watch carefully for a short concrete track dropping to the left, which joins a grassy track leading to a road junction. Turn left at the junction to return to the start of the walk on the coast road at **Rocquaine Bay**.

Rocks and reefs exposed beyond the northernmost coast of Guernsey

Pointe de la Moye is the southernmost
point on the coast of Guernsey

Distance	63.5km (39 miles)
Terrain	Almost entirely coastal, including busy and quiet roads, tracks and paths, ranging from urban areas to cliff-tops, sand dunes, woods and commons. Beach walking is an option, depending on the tides.
Start/Finish	Liberation Monument, St Peter Port
Refreshments	Pubs, restaurants, cafés, kiosks and shops are available at many points around the coast.
Transport	All the bus services on Guernsey start and finish at St Peter Port and most of them reach the coast at some other point. The 7 and 7A services run along or near the coast all the way round the island.

There is no doubt that most of the best scenery on Guernsey is around the coast. Naturally, many walkers feel obliged to concentrate their explorations along the coastline, and fortunately there is good access almost all the way. Once a year, in the middle of summer, there is an organised charity walk around the entire coast of the island. As the coast is well-served by bus routes, walkers with plenty of time to spare should split the distance over three or four days and take the time to enjoy the experience.

A complete route description is unnecessary here, as the coastal route is described a stretch at a time, in a clockwise direction, ranging from Walk 2 to Walk 14 throughout this guidebook. However, the following notes help to join all the short sections together, and your daily stages can be planned simply by adding up several short stretches to reach a distance that is comfortable and achievable. The assumption is that you will start from St Peter Port, walk in a clockwise direction round the coast, and finish back in town. However, as the walk is circular, any point serves perfectly well for the start and finish, and there is no bar on walking anticlockwise, though all the route directions would need

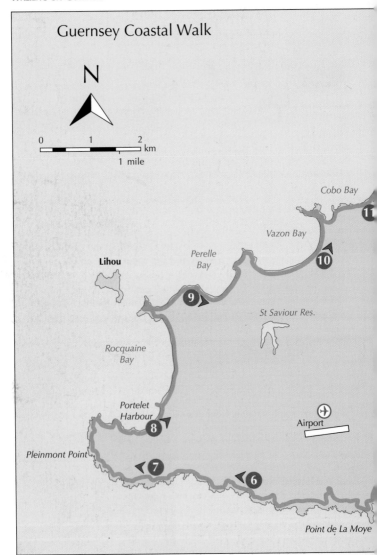

Guernsey Coastal Walk

N

0   1   2 km
1 mile

Cobo Bay

Vazon Bay

Perelle Bay

Lihou

St Saviour Res.

Rocquaine Bay

Portelet Harbour

Pleinmont Point

Airport

Point de La Moye

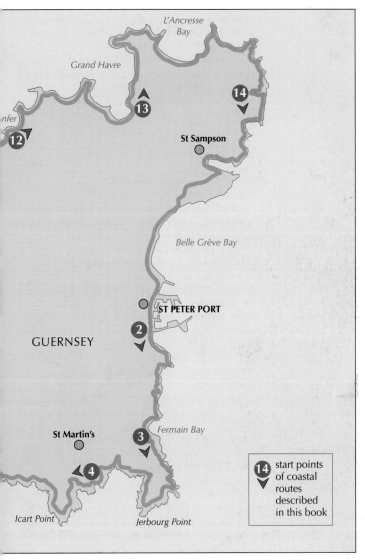

L'Ancresse
Bay

Grand Havre

nfer

St Sampson

Belle Grève Bay

ST PETER PORT

GUERNSEY

St Martin's

Fermain Bay

Icart Point

Jerbourg Point

14 start points
of coastal
routes
described
in this book

to be reversed. Bear in mind that any optional extensions mentioned increase the distance, and may be dependent on the tide being out.

A leisurely three-day walk around the coast could start at St Peter Port and be split at Mont Hèrault and Port Soif, or at least split somewhere before or after those points. Bus services allow easy exits from the route and an easy return the following day. In the middle of summer, Itex and the Rotary Club organise a gruelling one-day walk around the coast of Guernsey, attracting hundreds of walkers who are sponsored for charity.

Walk 2 St Peter Port to Fermain Bay
4km (2½ miles)
Start at the Liberation Monument in St Peter Port and walk beside the harbour to reach La Vallette. Follow woodland paths fairly close to the coast to reach Fermain Bay.

Walk 3 Fermain Bay to Moulin Huet Bay
5km (3 miles)
Follow the route description from Fermain Bay, out of the woods and around the open cliff-tops of Jerbourg Point. Unless descents are made to beaches along the way, stay high until a descent is made to Moulin Huet Bay.

Walk 4 Moulin Huet Bay to Petit Bôt Bay
5km (3 miles)
Follow the route description from Moulin Huet Bay and decide whether to visit Saints Bay, or stay high to walk round Icart Point. Pass above Jaonnet Bay, and later drop down into a wooded valley to reach Petit Bôt Bay.

Walk 5 Petit Bôt Bay to La Prévôte
5km (3 miles)
Follow the route description from Petit Bôt Bay, along a fine stretch of cliffs to Pointe de la Moye and Le Gouffre. A series of ascents and descents feature as the cliff path is followed to a German Observation Tower at La Prévôte.

Walk 6 La Prévôte to Mont Hèrault
4km (2½ miles)
Follow the route description from La Prévôte, along cliffs overlooking rugged coves and headlands, to Mont Hèrault. This is a good day's walk from St Peter Port and there is a bus service just inland.

Walk 7 Mont Hèrault to Portelet Harbour
4km (2½ miles)
Follow the route description as the coast path turns round the Pleinmont headland at the south-western point of Guernsey. Pass huge German observation towers before descending to Portelet Harbour.

Walk 8 Portelet Harbour to La Rocque
5km (3 miles)
Follow the route description round Rocquaine Bay, seldom straying more than a few paces from a coastal road. Lihou Island can be visited as an optional extra at low water during spring tides.

Taking a break on low granite outcrops on the west coast of Guernsey

A pink carpet of thrift on the coast near Mont Cuet on the northern coast of Guernsey

Walk 9 La Rocque to Vazon
3km (2 miles)

Follow the route description, either using the coastal road or walking on the beach round Perelle Bay and Richmond. Many stretches along the beach are rough and rocky. Easier walking follows around Vazon Bay.

Walk 10 Vazon to Cobo
4km (2½ miles)

Follow the route description around Vazon Bay. Walk round the Hommet headland and a couple of smaller headlands, continuing onwards to reach Cobo Bay.

Walk 11 Cobo to Port Soif
2.5km (1½ miles)

Follow the route description and use either the coastal road or the beach round Cobo Bay. Walk round the headland at Grandes Rocques. Continue to Port Soif, which is a handy place to break the second day's walk.

Walk 12 Port Soif to Vale Parish Church

6km (3½ miles)

Follow the route description and use a low-level coastal path round bays and headlands, never far from the coastal road. The largest bay is the Grande Havre and the coastal path heads towards Vale Parish Church.

Walk 13 Vale Parish Church to Le Déhus Dolmen

9km (5½ miles)

Follow the route description around the northernmost parts of Guernsey, where the coastal path links defensive towers while turning round several headlands and bays. Head inland slightly to Le Déhus Dolmen.

Walk 14 Le Déhus Dolmen to St Peter Port

7km (4½ miles)

Follow the route description and walk round the harbour at St Sampson. Continue along the coast round Belle Grève Bay to finish back beside the Liberation Monument at St Peter Port.

THE ITEX–ROTARY WALK – GUERNSEY

This one-day event is held in the middle of summer and has been organised since 1997. Its format mirrors the 'Around the Island Walk' established in Jersey in 1991. Walkers raise funds for charity, and these days up to 500 people set off to complete the full distance, with many more joining for shorter stretches. The route is more or less the same as outlined above, running in a clockwise direction, but with slightly different start and finish points in St Peter Port, and some small headlands are omitted from the route. See www.itexwalk.gg.

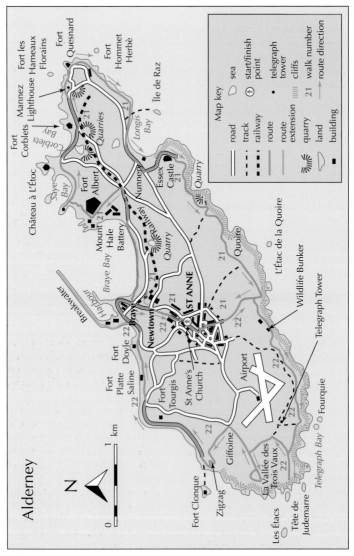

Alderney

N

0 __ 1 km

Map key

road		sea
track		start/finish point
railway		telegraph tower
route		cliffs
route extension		quarry
quarry	21	walk number
land	→	route direction
building		

Fort Quesnard
Fort les Hameaux Florains
Fort Hommet Herbé
Mannez Lighthouse
Fort Corblets
Corblets Bay
île de Raz
Longis Bay
Château à l'Étoc
Saye Bay
Quarries
Fort Albert
Mount Hale Battery
Nunnery
Essex Castle
Quarry
Quarry
Breakwater
Braye Bay
Quarry
Railway
Harbour
Quoire
L'Étac de la Quoire
ST ANNE
Wildlife Bunker
Braye
Newtown
Fort Doyle
Fort Platte Saline
St Anne's Church
Fort Tourgis
Airport
Telegraph Tower
Giffoine
La Vallée des Trois Vaux
Telegraph Bay
Fourquie
Fort Clonque
Zigzag
Les Étacs
Tête de Judemarre

21
22

ALDERNEY

A pointed outcrop of rock is a striking feature on the way to the lighthouse at the eastern end of Alderney

Alderney is the most far-flung of the Channel Islands, yet lies closer to both France and Britain than the others. The island's close proximity to France led to the construction of a large number of forts during the 19th century, particularly in response to the building of a naval base at Cherbourg in the 1840s. The forts were built on high ground, beside harbours and on little rocky islets. By the time they were all completed the threat of war and invasion had receded, and none was manned to full capacity. None of the forts is open as a visitor attraction. Some have been converted to private dwellings or holiday dwellings, or been turned over to industrial uses, while others are in ruins. Overall, the island looks like a monstrous stone-built battleship!

Immediately before the German Occupation, almost the entire population of the island was evacuated. The handful of people that remained were deported to Guernsey. With no native islanders to witness it, the Germans built three large concentration camps, constructed batteries at either end of the island and strengthened some of the existing forts. At the end of the war months passed before the islanders returned, allowing time for the concentration camps to be dismantled. All the properties on the island had been ransacked and the islanders faced the enormous task of reconstructing their community.

For some decades the harbour was unsuitable for ferry traffic, but the area has been completely renovated and more services may be provided in future. Most visitors arrive by air, and the airport takes up a huge amount of space. Flights between Guernsey, Alderney and Britain are operated by Aurigny, www.aurigny.com and Blue Islands, www.blueislands.com. There are no ferries from Guernsey to Alderney, but Manche Îles Express, www.manche-iles-express.com, serves the island from Diélette in France. There is no need for transport on the island, though there is a peculiar railway service, occasional tour buses and taxis.

For tourist information, check with Visit Alderney, States of Alderney, PO Box 1, Alderney, GY9 3AA, tel. 01481 822811, www.visitalderney.com.

Masses of flowers cover a slope overlooking a rock stack on the way towards Telegraph Tower

WALK 21

Alderney – East

Distance	12km (7½ miles)
Terrain	Coastal roads, tracks and paths, reaching cliff-tops later.
Start/Finish	St Anne's Parish Church
Refreshments	Plenty in St Anne and at Braye Harbour. Campsite shop at Saye Bay.
Transport	Taxis are available, but are unnecessary.

A walk round the eastern half of Alderney passes several old fortifications, with glimpses of the only working railway in the Channel Islands. The fortifications range from stout, sprawling structures on headlands to small, compact forts on little islets, supplemented by masses of German Occupation bunkers. It is sobering to remember that the Germans converted Alderney into a concentration camp, whose full history may never be revealed. Almost all traces were removed after the war, before any of the islanders were allowed home. Alderney has some of the broadest country roads in the Channel Islands, which is strange as there is very little traffic.

The main shopping street in **St Anne** is the cobbled Victoria Street. Follow it downhill from St Anne's Parish Church and turn left and right in quick succession at a junction to pass Alderney Methodist Church. A narrow road leads past the Belle Vue Bar and cricket ground, then a path can be followed downhill, keeping right to join the lower part of Braye Road. Follow the road across a railway line to reach **Braye Harbour**. There are toilets and places offering food and drink. ▶

See map on page 150

Alderney Railway is the only working railway in the Channel Islands and trains run from Braye Harbour to Mannez Quarry. The railway was founded in 1847, but has not seen continuous service. It was constructed to move stone across Alderney during the construction of the breakwater. The engine is diesel and the carriages

An optional extension is a walk along the massive restored 19th century stone breakwater, measuring just over 2km (1¼ miles) there and back.

153

are ex-London Underground, connecting with a miniature railway at Mannez Quarry. The railway runs mainly at weekends, Easter to September, tel. 01481 822978, **www.alderneyrailway.com**.

If you choose not to walk along the breakwater, simply turn right to follow a road, Rue de Beaumont, around **Braye Bay**, passing the tiny Braye Road Railway Station. The road and railway part company, and there is no need to walk on the road as there is a fine grassy crescent, as well as a splendid sandy beach when the tide is out. Whether walking on the grass or the beach, the road has to be joined later and is followed as it rises inland.

Do not turn left down the road serving **Mount Hale Battery**, but turn left up the track serving **Fort Albert** and enjoy the fine views over Braye Bay and the breakwater. Follow a narrow path down to a small fortified headland and **Saye Bay**. Either walk round the sandy bay if the tide is out, or follow a track a short way inland, through a gate to walk behind dunes covered in marram grass, and

The sandy beach at Braye Bay is backed by grassy dunes and overlooks the Breakwater

through a field used as a campsite. ▶ Either way, join a road that crosses over a small tunnel, and follow it round a headland where **Château à L'Etoc** stands as a private residence.

Continue along the road round **Corblets Bay**, which is attractively sandy and rocky, passing a headland where **Fort Corblets** is another private residence. There is a fine spike of rock to the left on the way to a prominent black and white lighthouse. Keep to a path on the seaward side of Mannez Lighthouse, which was built in 1912, overlooking a little islet crowned by the ruins of **Fort les Hameaux Florains**. Follow the road to **Fort Quesnard**, yet another conversion into a private residence. Drift left along a track signposted for Longis Bay, which becomes a ribbon of grass round a flowery headland. There are a few houses just inland, while out on a rocky islet are the ruins of **Fort Houmet Herbè**. This is the nearest point in the Channel Islands to France, which may be visible across the sea only 9 miles (14km) away. ▶ Follow the grassy coastal path to reach a tall, thick concrete sea wall around **Longis Bay**. Decide whether to follow a track across a grassy area inland, or walk along the sandy beach while the tide is out. A concrete tidal causeway offers access to an old fort on **Île de Raz**, again while the tide is out. At the end of Longis Bay there is a slipway, toilets and a fortified house. ▶ Follow a road a short way up a partly wooded valley, then turn left as if approaching the Longis Bay Garden Centre. The road, marked 'no through road', climbs to **Essex Castle**, offering fine views back round Longis Bay to the eastern end of Alderney. Just before reaching the hill-top fort, head left along a grassy track. Keep left to follow another track and then a narrower cliff path. The surroundings become more and more flowery and there are good views along the cliffs.

When a road is reached there is an unsightly refuse tip in an old quarry. Turn right up the road, then left along another track. This again becomes a narrow path flanked by tall vegetation. Further along, before reaching the prominent sea-stack of **L'Étac de la Quoire**, the path is diverted right, inland, then left at a junction. Follow

Snacks may be available if the campsite shop is open.

This stretch of sea is known as The Race and always shows signs of turbulence.

The house is usually called the 'Nunnery', and it may be built on a Roman foundation.

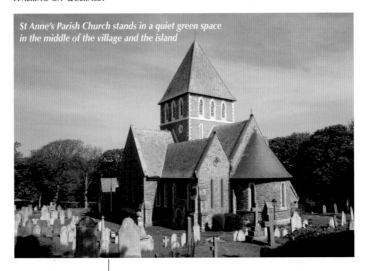

St Anne's Parish Church stands in a quiet green space in the middle of the village and the island

It is possible to continue round the cliff coast, with reference to Walk 22, making a complete circuit around Alderney.

a grassy track straight onwards and turn right, inland, at the next junction. ◀ The track passes through fields, then heads straight down a tarmac road called La Brecque Philippe. As you enter the village of **St Anne**, turn left along a cobbled street called Le Bourgage and quickly right down a narrow street called Venelle Sergente. Turn left along the High Street and turn right down Victoria Street to return to the parish church.

The **Alderney Museum** is tucked away in an old school building off High Street, behind an old clock tower which is all that remains of the previous parish church. Exhibits have a strongly nautical theme throughout, as befits an island, ranging from archaeological artefacts to German Occupation memorabilia. The museum is run by the Alderney Society, and there is an entry charge, **www.alderneysociety.org**.

WALK 22
Alderney – West

Distance	12km (7½ miles)
Terrain	Tracks and cliff paths, with some road walking towards the end.
Start/Finish	St Anne's Parish Church
Refreshments	Plenty in St Anne and at Braye Harbour.
Transport	Taxis are available but are unnecessary.

Alderney Airport takes up a lot of space, including all the highest ground in the west. The cliff coast on that side of the island is very approachable and overlooks a series of spiky sea stacks. A variety of tracks and paths can be linked, while a road passes a number of fortifications, both on Alderney and on nearby islets. This walk runs clockwise from St Anne, round the south-west cliff coast to Braye Harbour and its breakwater, before heading back up to St Anne.

The village of **St Anne** is the only real settlement on Alderney, usually referred to as 'Town'. Its stone houses and narrow, cobbled streets are delightful, and traffic is quite limited. St Anne's Parish Church is like a tiny cathedral and dates only from 1850, replacing an earlier structure whose clock tower now survives at the Alderney Museum on High Street. Most of the island's shops are on Victoria Street. The post office supplies Alderney stamps, though Guernsey stamps may be used when posting items. The amount of whitewash expended on the buildings makes the town a dazzling sight in bright sunlight.

See map on page 150

The main shopping street in **St Anne** is the cobbled Victoria Street. Follow it uphill and turn left along High Street. Turn right up a narrow street called Venelle Sergente, turn left along the cobbled street called Le Bourgage, then right to follow a road called La Brecque

157

Philippe. This leaves St Anne and gives way to a track, becoming grassy as it runs through fields. Turn right to follow a fine cliff path, crossing a dip that can be muddy when wet, passing in front of a large building. There is access to a 'Wildlife Bunker', in a concrete bunker built during the German Occupation. Another dip in the path is quite wooded, before reaching a broad track.

There are two ways to continue. The easiest is to follow the track, which is broad and clear, surfaced in tarmac where it crosses a couple of dips, and often flanked by masses of gorse. A tougher alternative is to follow a narrow path closer to the cliffs, marked by occasional white stones. This is highly recommended on a clear day and there are ways back onto the track. Either way, keep an eye on the **Telegraph Tower** ahead, which is a notable landmark. If following the track, turn left before reaching the tower to follow another track towards the cliffs, then turn right to explore along the cliff path. ◄

Paths run along the cliff tops and the views around Telegraph Bay are among the wildest and rockiest on

There is a view of the distant islet of Coque Lihou, as well as two rock stacks closer to hand – Fourquie and La Nache.

Flowery cliff-tops overlook a series of rock stacks and the more distant islet of Coque Lihou

WALK 22 – ALDERNEY – WEST

Alderney. There is less gorse, and a greater expanse of flowers along the way. Reaching Tête de Judemarre, a long flight of steps leads down into **Telegraph Bay**, but these have become unsafe and are closed to visitors. Another decision needs to be made about how to continue.

La Vallée des Trois Vaux is a significant gap in the cliff line. There is a narrow path leading down into it, then straight up the other side, but the way is arduous. Alternatively, follow a path and track inland, turn left along a broad track close to the airport runway, turning left again at a junction where a signpost indicates 'The Gannets'. Follow the track, which is flanked by gorse, where Dartford warblers and peregrines have been spotted. The track ends in a broad loop overlooking **Les Étacs**. These pyramidal stacks are snow-white with bird-lime and a large, raucous colony of gannets is in possession of the place – one of Europe's most southerly colonies. ▶

Follow the track inland past a number of concrete structures, all part of a coastal battery built during the

Les Étacs are covered in bird lime and are home to vast numbers of raucous gannets

The nearby cliffs feature fulmar, kittiwake, shag, guillemot, razorbill and gulls.

German Occupation. Continue straight along a road at
Giffoine, which leads to a road junction. Turn left along
a track signposted as 'Zigzag'. Turn right along another
track within a few paces and follow this down zigzags
on a steep slope. From this vantage point, overlooking
The Swinge, the sea looks disturbed even on a calm day,
as conflicting currents cause standing waves and eddies
between projecting rocks. Fort Clonque can be seen out
on a rocky islet, linked to Alderney by a concrete tidal
causeway; it is now holiday accommodation. The large
island out to sea is Burhou, an important breeding site
for puffins and storm petrels, and part of an extensive
'Ramsar' reserve.

Turn right to follow a clear track along the coast,
passing close to a couple of houses, then walking round
the foot of **Fort Tourgis**. At the time of writing, planning
permission had been granted to convert the fort into a
luxury hotel.

There are some German concrete bunkers below the
fort. A road is joined, but a track branches off to the left,
passing **Fort Platte Saline**, running towards Fort Doyle,
both of which have been converted to industrial uses.
Follow a path through a little cutting to pass **Fort Doyle**
then walk beside a road to reach **Braye Harbour**. There
are toilets and places offering food and drink. An optional
extension is a walk along the massive, restored 19th
century stone breakwater, measuring just over 2km (1¼
miles) there and back.

BRAYE HARBOUR

Originally, Alderney's main harbour was at Longis Bay, but trade and com-
merce shifted to Braye after a jetty was built in 1736. The current breakwater
was commenced in 1847, when a naval base was planned for the island.
The original plan was to have two breakwaters enclosing the harbour, but
the second one was never built. While the breakwater offers a good measure
of protection to Braye Harbour, it is by no means proof against storms and
the sea sometimes surges over the top of it. It has suffered extensive damage
in the past, but has recently been restored.

Gulls abound around the coast of Alderney

Turning inland from the harbour, the tiny Braye Road Railway Station is passed on the Alderney Railway. ▶ Braye Road runs straight uphill to return to **St Anne**, but it is also possible to use a path off to the right of the road, which climbs a rugged slope to reach a cricket ground and the Belle Vue Bar. A quick left and right turn at the Alderney Methodist Church leads straight back onto Victoria Street, where the walk started.

See Walk 21 for details.

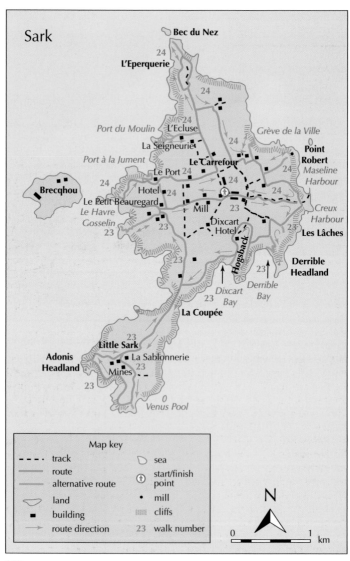

Sark

Bec du Nez

L'Eperquerie

Port du Moulin — L'Ecluse

Grève de la Ville

La Seigneurie

Le Carrefour

Point Robert

Maseline Harbour

Port à la Jument

Le Port

Brecqhou

Hotel

Le Petit Beauregard

Le Havre Gosselin

Mill

Dixcart Hotel

Creux Harbour

Les Lâches

Hogsback

Derrible Headland

Dixcart Bay

Derrible Bay

La Coupée

Little Sark

Adonis Headland

La Sablonnerie

Mines

Venus Pool

Map key

- - - track
—— route
—— alternative route
⬭ land
▪ building
→ route direction

⬭ sea
✚ start/finish point
• mill
||||| cliffs
23 walk number

N

0 — 1 km

SARK

The rugged stacks of Les Autolets, with Sark to the left and Brecqhou to the right

Sark has been settled for a long time, dating back to pre-history, but by no means continuously. St Magloire, a cousin of St Sampson, is associated with a settlement dating from the 6th century. For over 1000 years pirates sometimes used the island as a base. The French held it from time to time, notably from 1549 to 1553. In 1565 Helier de Carteret of Jersey, along with 40 families, made a concerted attempt to settle the island and oversee its defence by raising a militia force from the population. This arrangement was granted Royal approval and the island parliament, known as the Chief Pleas, was established, with a feudal Seigneur as its head. There were never any large-scale fortifications on the island, only a handful of old cannons mounted on headlands.

The Sark Militia was disbanded in the 1880s. One wonders what they would have made of an attempted military coup in 1991. Andre Gardes, an unemployed French nuclear physicist, arrived on Sark armed with a semi-automatic weapon, announcing his intention to take control of the island. He was disarmed and arrested

163

The northernmost point of Sark, which breaks into islets and rocks with the advancing tide

by the island constable. The Seigneur missed this drama, being away on business in Guernsey for the day.

After 450 years of feudal government Sark finally embraced democracy and held a general election in December 2008. The Seigneur holds a position within the government and matters of state can be viewed on the Chief Pleas of Sark website, www. gov.sark.gg.

Sark is usually approached by ferry from Guernsey, with sailings operated by the Isle of Sark Shipping Company, www.sarkshipping company.com. There are also ferries from Jersey, operated by the French ferry company Manche Îles Express, www.manche-iles-express.com. There are no flights.

For tourist information and accommodation, check www.sark.info.

WALK 23
Sark – South

Distance	15km (9½ miles)
Terrain	Cliff paths, occasionally rugged, with other paths and broad tracks inland.
Start/Finish	The Avenue, The Village
Refreshments	Occasional pubs and tea gardens, mostly around The Village, but also on Little Sark.
Transport	Tractors and horse-drawn carriages are available, but are unnecessary.

Sark is entirely cliff-bound and while there is not a continuous cliff path round the island, short stretches of cliff path can be linked with other paths and tracks further inland. Sark has a skeleton network of dirt roads and tracks, where vehicles are limited to tractors, horse-drawn carriages and bicycles. The route described wanders round the southern half of the island, visiting Little Sark by way of a remarkable arête at La Coupée. A short circular path leads round rugged headlands, overlooking rocky coves.

The Avenue is the main shopping street in **The Village** in the middle of Sark. Follow a dirt road as if going to the harbour, but pick up a footpath from the Bel Air Inn. The path runs parallel to the road down through a wooded valley. Towards the bottom another path is signposted on the right, up a flight of steps. When the path reaches a bend on a track, it is worth making a short detour to the left, down a grassy path for a view overlooking **Creux Harbour**. Follow the track uphill and inland, later making another short detour left to **Les Lâches**, where a cannon stands on top of the cliffs. Follow the track inland, but before reaching a huddle of farm buildings, turn left through a small gate where a signpost points to Derrible and the Hogsback. A decision needs to be made at a small cliff-top duck-pond.

See map on page 162

Optional Extension to Derrible Bay

A strenuous optional detour can be made by turning left. A path starts easily, then steep, winding steps lead down to Derrible Bay. A small sandy beach is reached, flanked by cliffs. All those steps need to be climbed to return to the duck-pond. The distance is an additional 500m.

Look out for fulmars and peregrines.

◄ The other path from the duck-pond leads down into a little wooded valley and up the other side. Turn left at a path junction to make a detour onto the **Hogsback**, following a clear path between bushes to reach an old cannon, where there are dramatic views of the nearby cliffs and bays. Retrace your steps to the path junction and walk inland to reach a junction with a track. Walk straight across this junction to pick up and follow a path signposted for Dixcart Bay.

Walk down through a wooded valley, full of blue-bells and wild garlic in spring, staying on the clearest path while passing a house. Emerge from the woods and go down steps to reach the pebbly **Dixcart Bay**, where a small rock arch leans against a cliff. Walk back up into the woods and turn left at a path junction, rising from the woods across a steep, flowery slope. ◄ Watch for a stile between two gates on the left. Follow a fence alongside a field and cross another stile. A path flanked by bushes runs down through a small wooded area, then rises across a flowery slope with good views, joining a dirt road. Turn left to cross the steep-sided rugged arête at **La Coupée**, admiring splendid views on both sides.

A track at the top leads inland to the Dixcart Hotel, if food and drink are required.

This knife-edged arête, **La Coupée**, connecting Sark and Little Sark, is one of the most admired points on this walk. A plaque records: 'In 1945 this roadway was rebuilt in concrete and handrails added by German prisoner-of-war labour working under the direction of 259 Field Company Royal Engineers.' There are fine views of Herm, Guernsey, Jersey and sometimes the coast of France. Take care while crossing, watching for tractors and horse-drawn carriages. Cyclists are supposed to walk across, but many of them ride across at speed!

A horse and carriage crosses from Sark to Little
Sark along the airy road at La Coupée

The view from southern Sark towards Guernsey
from a headland near the derelict Silver Mines

Follow the dirt road as it rises from La Coupée onto **Little Sark**, descending towards a huddle of houses around **La Sablonnerie**, where the hotel dates from the 16th century. Food and drink are available here, as well as at a tea garden next door. Now follows a splendid circular walk!

Turn left to follow a track between La Sablonnerie and the tea garden, and keep left at a farm. A gate on the right is marked 'private', but signposts on the other side indicate Venus Pool and the Silver Mines. Keep left for the Venus Pool, and the path passes a chimney-like air shaft associated with the Hope Mine.

Hope Mine was established by the Seigneur, Ernest Le Pelley following the discovery of silver in 1836. He raised funds to exploit the silver by mortgaging his property to a privateer, Jean Allaire, who owned Jethou. The venture was a financial disaster, Le Pelley lost everything, and Allaire's daughter became the Seigneure!

Follow a path winding down past gorse bushes to a rocky headland overlooking **Venus Pool**. ▶ When you are ready climb back uphill, but turn left at a bench to follow another path round the headland. The path climbs towards the old air shaft, but do not go that far. Instead, note two paths on the left. The first should be avoided, since it only descends to the rocky shore. The other path runs through bushes and crosses a stile, then makes its way round rugged headlands. For the most part the path is flanked by gorse bushes and is quite obvious. When it crosses a stile into a field, keep left and cross another stile later. Take the time to walk onto the **Adonis Headland** to enjoy fine views.

The path continues round the coast but eventually reaches a dead-end at a bench and fine viewpoint. Cross a stile beforehand into a field, cross another stile into another field then climb to reach a gate leading onto a grassy track. Follow the track further inland and it becomes sandy as it passes through a lovely farmyard. The next buildings along the track are the hotel and tea

Offshore, L'Étac is colonised by puffin, manx shearwater, shag, guillemot, razorbill, terns and gulls.

garden at **La Sablonnerie**. Continue straight along the dirt road, back across the remarkable gap at **La Coupée**.

After following the dirt road over a broad rise, a crossroads is reached where a track on the right leads to Dixcart Hotel. However, turn left and follow a grassy track beside a field and later turn left and keep left of a thatched cottage. A track leads to a prominent obelisk, the Pilcher Monument.

Optional Extension to Le Havre Gosselin

If time can be spared for another optional detour, follow a rugged path downhill, winding further down flights of steps to reach a rock-bound harbour between Sark and Brecqhou, called Le Havre Gosselin. Climb all the way back to the monument and follow the track inland to continue. The distance there and back is 500m.

> The little island of **Brecqhou** is separated from Sark by the narrow, rock-walled Gouliot Passage. Brecqhou is owned by property-dealing twins, the Barclay brothers. A modern castle and other buildings have been erected on the island. The brothers often bid for property on Sark – a contentious issue if you talk to people on the island about it. Access to Brecqhou is forbidden, but it can be viewed from nearby headlands, or from a passing boat or ferry.

Alternatively, keep left of Le Petit Beauregard and continue round Sark with reference to Walk 24.

Simply keep to the clearest track, passing left of the thatched cottage, turning right at Le Petit Beauregard to continue inland. ◄ When a staggered dirt crossroads is reached, turn quickly right and left. The dirt road passes a windmill tower dating from 1571, which was used as an observation tower during the German Occupation. It stands on the highest point on Sark at 111m (365ft). There is a dip in the road before it rises into **The Village**, passing a visitor centre. A number of places offer food and drink along The Avenue. ◄

Tough walkers can complete a circuit all the way round Sark in a day by linking the coastal sections of Walks 23 and 24.

At the harbour below the Pilcher Monument, looking across to the gap between Sark and Brecqhou

WALK 24

Sark – North

Distance	10km (6¼ miles)
Terrain	Broad tracks and cliff paths. Some of the cliff paths are quite rugged.
Start/Finish	The Avenue, The Village
Refreshments	Pubs and tea gardens around The Village. Also bars or cafés at the Hotel Petit Champ, Island Hall and La Seigneurie.
Transport	Tractors and horse-drawn carriages are available, but are unnecessary.

There isn't a continuous cliff path round Sark, but there are plenty of paths offering there-and-back walks to rugged bays and headlands. The walk around the northern half of the island sometimes follows dirt roads well inland, but every so often there are splendid paths to the coast. The gardens of La Seigneurie are passed, while the Sark Occupation and Heritage Museum could be visited at the beginning or end of the walk.

See map on page 162

See Walk 23 for information.

The Avenue is the main shopping street in **The Village** in the middle of Sark. Follow the dirt road past the shops and post office, keeping left to pass the visitor centre. There is a slight dip in the road, which then rises to pass a windmill tower dating from 1571, which was used as an observation tower during the German Occupation. It stands on the highest point on Sark at 111m (365ft). When a staggered crossroads is reached, turn quickly right and left. Follow the track to **Le Petit Beauregard**, turn right through a gateway, then left to follow a track through another gate. This grassy track passes gorse bushes and reaches a rocky headland overlooking the small island of **Brecqhou**. ◄

On the way to the headland, note another path heading right, rising across a slope of gorse. Follow this alongside a vegetated bank or stone wall, and a couple of grassy tracks are seen heading inland. Either of these can be followed and both lead to a gap between fields, flanked by benches. Go through a gate to the left of this gap, turn left alongside a field, and go through another gate to follow a track onwards.

Optional Extension to Port à la Jument

On the left, signposted as 'Path to Port à la Jument', is an optional detour. A path leads down steps, turning right to pass an old winch above a steep and rugged slope. Rise a little among bushes then descend steeply on the grassy slope, maybe with bluebells alongside. Steps continue downhill, passing a rock-step, finally winding down to Port à la Jument, where the beach is made of big boulders. Steps have to be retraced and the distance there and back is 500m.

If the detour is not taken, follow the track to a farm at **Le Port**. Hotel Petit Champ is off to the right if food and drink are required; otherwise follow the bendy track further inland. Keep straight ahead when a broader track is reached, passing the Sark Methodist Church and a shop. The track crosses a broad rise almost in the centre of Sark, passing the Millennium Field and Island Hall, which has a café/bar. Turn left at a crossroads, signposted for **La Seigneurie**. ▸

The gardens at La Seigneurie are generally open daily from April to October, and there is an entry charge, tel. 01481 832208. There is also a café. The Seigneurie itself, dating from 1730, is not open to the public.

Optional Extension to Port du Moulin

Beyond La Seigneurie, a track on the left is signposted for 'Window in the Rock' and 'Port du Moulin', which can be reached by an optional detour. The track leads to L'Ecluse, where a path runs into woodland. Turn down to the left; then when the path splits, walk straight ahead to reach the 'Window in the Rock'. This is exactly what the name suggests – a hole cut into solid rock, so don't walk straight off the cliff edge, just admire the view and retrace your steps! Take the other path down steps to reach another junction. Right leads down to the rugged Port du Moulin, while left climbs and winds onto a rocky hilltop offering splendid coastal views. Whatever options are chosen, retrace your steps back to L'Ecluse and the main dirt road. The distance there and back, covering all options, is 2km (1¼ miles).

Looking back along the coast, the stacks of Les Autelets look amazing and are home to a large population of guillemots.

Follow the dirt road straight onwards and northwards, to its very end above the wild and rugged headland of **L'Eperquerie**. The headland is encircled by lovely narrow paths. Keep to the left to pick up the first of these, passing between banks of gorse and enjoying swathes of flowers on the rugged slopes. ◀ A spur path leads to the very end of the headland, but the attractive rocky islets at **Bec du Nez** can only be reached when the tide is out by scrambling over rocks.

Backtrack along the spur path, but keep left to explore the other side of the headland, passing an old cannon on the way. At this point, paths need to be followed to the right to climb back up to the dirt road. Heading left leads down to a landing place.

This later runs fairly straight back towards The Village, if a rapid finish to the walk is required.

Follow the dirt road back to a junction and turn left, then keep right at another junction near an attractive thatched house, following a rather bendy stretch of track. ◀ A crossroads, **Le Carrefour**, is reached and the full walk continues by turning left, signposted for Grève de la Ville and the lighthouse. Turn right at the next junction, following the track as it bends right to yet another junction.

Optional Extension to Grève de la Ville

For an optional detour to Grève de la Ville, turn left to follow a grassy path down beside a wood, later winding down to the shore. Boats are often moored at Grève de la Ville. You need to retrace your steps back uphill; the distance there and back is 1km (½mile).

If the detour isn't made, simply turn right at the junction, along a bendy track, to reach another junction.

Optional Extension to Point Robert

At this point, another optional detour is available by turning left. The track drops to cross a dip, then climbs, turning left and right as marked. However, note that there is no access to the lighthouse on Point Robert, although views can be enjoyed from the cliff-top. Retrace your steps to the junction and turn left to continue. The distance there and back is almost 1km (½ mile).

Looking along the north-west coast of Sark from a rugged path near the Window in the Rock

Follow the track onwards, keeping straight ahead at a junction. ▸ The track later turns left and a signpost indicates 'Footpath to Harbours'. Note that the path is alongside a field, not along the track. At the bottom of the field a little gate gives access to woods, and a short climb offers a fine view of the **Maseline Harbour**. The path runs down and up before dropping down to the road near the harbour. Turn left to visit the harbour, or right to walk uphill and inland. ▸ If choosing the latter, follow the path running through the wooded valley parallel to the road up Harbour Hill, reaching the Bel Air Inn at the top. A dirt road runs straight back through **The Village** to finish.

Turning right at the junction gives a short cut to The Village.

Alternatively, climb up steps to continue around the island with reference to Walk 23.

The delightful white sands of Shell Beach on the north-eastern side of Herm

HERM

Herm is a real gem of an island, small enough to explore thoroughly, yet large enough to occupy a walker for most of a day. There are prehistoric sites dotted around Herm, but the island has not been continually inhabited. St Tugual, who lived in the 6th century, is associated with the island, although little is known about him. There may have been a chapel on Herm as early as the 6th century, but the current church is believed to date from the 12th century. Herm has had many owners or tenants over the centuries and practically all of them have been documented. It was probably busiest when quarrying developed from 1815, employing as many as 400 people a few years later. The tough 'Herm Granite' is actually granodiorite.

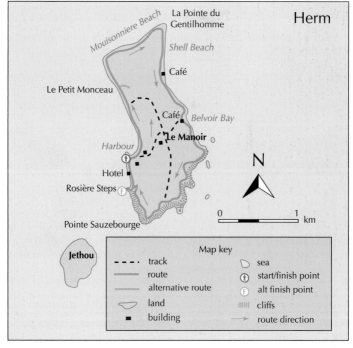

177

Leaving the Harbour on Herm and following a track past charming buildings and gardens

Herm was spared brutal fortification during the German Occupation, but at the same time all its buildings fell into ruins. Practically all the credit for the development of Herm since 1949 goes to the Wood and Heyworth families. The overgrown, abandoned island was transformed into a delightful place featuring charming walks and wonderful scenery, offering food, drink and accommodation in a tranquil

setting. John and Julia Singer took over the tenancy of Herm in 2008, vowing to maintain the island as a quiet and beautiful place for visitors to enjoy.

Herm is reached by ferry from Guernsey, Travel Trident, tel. 01481 721379 (Guernsey) or 01481 722377 (Herm). For tourist information and accommodation on the island, visit the Administration Office, www. herm.com.

WALK 25

Herm

Distance	6.5km (4 miles)
Terrain	Easy coastal paths and tracks.
Start/Finish	The Harbour
Refreshments	Hotel, pub and beach cafés.
Transport	None, nor is any needed.

A complete coastal walk around the island is easily achieved; it is remarkably varied and immensely satisfying. Good paths lead from the harbour, round a sandy, grassy common and along a fine cliff path, offering a complete circular tour. Tracks criss-cross through the middle of the island, and at no point are walkers ever more than half-an-hour's walk from the harbour. Food, drink and accommodation are readily available and, although space is limited, there are actually some fine open spaces to be enjoyed.

Depending on the state of the tides, this walk will start either at the **Harbour**, or at the Rosière Steps. ▶ The building closest to the Harbour is the Administration Office, and there is a most comprehensive signpost alongside. To the right is the Ship Inn and White House Hotel. Straight uphill is St Tugual's Church and Le Manoir. To the left, the way this route goes, is the post office, gift shops, Mermaid Tavern, restaurant, toilets and campsite.

If the landing is at Rosière Steps, climb up the steps and follow a fine track to the Harbour.

A broad path runs along the coast, with dense growths of aloes alongside. The path reaches a tiny cemetery and forks. Heading right allows a short-cut across the island; but otherwise keep left to hug the grassy coast past **Le Petit Monceau**. ▶ Follow the narrow path round the north coast of the island, or walk along the **Mouisonniere Beach**. If walking onshore, there are areas of bracken, thorny burnet rose, sea holly and marram grass. A slender stone monument called Pierre aux Râts is a landmark on the way to **La Pointe du Gentilhomme**.

In 2010 this rugged little hill was crowned with an Antony Gormley sculpture, 'Another Time', one of 100 sculptures positioned around the world.

See map on page 177

179

Le Petit Monceau suddenly sprouted an Antony Gormley sculpture in 2010

Again, either follow paths or walk on the sand while enjoying the popular **Shell Beach**. There is a beach café at the far end.

A track runs above and behind the beach café, across a slope of bracken, brambles, bushes and flowers. Toilets are passed before the track turns a point and overlooks **Belvoir Bay**. There is another beach café here, as well as a coast-to-coast track running straight over the top of the island back to the **Harbour**. Continue along the coast, following a narrow path up steps, broadening as it crosses a steep, flowery slope above a rocky coast. After turning around a rocky point overlooking an islet, the path rises and undulates across flowery slopes with fine cliff views. Pass a fenced-off rocky chasm and follow another undulating stretch, then a short flight of steps leads downhill. ▶

The path turns round **Point Sauzebourge**, which is a fine viewpoint for the little island of Jethou, a favourite haunt for puffins. Go down a flight of steps, and just to the left at the bottom are the **Rosière Steps**. If your ferry is scheduled to leave from here, bear this location in mind; otherwise keep right and follow a good track back to the **Harbour**.

Note a fine track here, running south to north through the middle of Herm, passing Le Manoir.

Bréhon Tower is seen to good effect on the ferry from St Peter Port to Herm. It stands on a rock in the stretch of water known as the Little Russel. It was the last gun tower to be built in the Channel Islands, dating from 1856, and was built in response to the naval base which was being established at Cherbourg in France. The elliptical structure had four guns on top and contained a large reserve of ammunition, food and fresh water.

The Channel Islands Way extends to Jersey and makes a complete coastal circuit round the island

APPENDIX A

The Channel Islands Way

The Channel Islands Way was the happy inspiration of a flute-playing trio on Jersey, while enjoying a meal and good red wine after practising together in 2005. Jennifer Bridge had enjoyed a series of walks during one of the Jersey Walking Weeks, all of them led by Blue Badge guide Arthur Lamy, while Andrew Goodyear and Anna Heuston had enjoyed a trek along the celebrated West Highland Way in Scotland. As the wine flowed and their conversation developed, they agreed that a long-distance, island-hopping Channel Islands Way would be a truly remarkable route. A few years later, the idea was put to tourism bodies around the islands and was received with enthusiasm.

The mapping and a route description was prepared by Arthur Lamy. A guidebook has been published by Coast, and a Channel Islands Way website is also planned. The route envisages walkers making an anti-clockwise circuit round the coast of Jersey, and clockwise circuits round the coasts of Guernsey, Alderney, Sark and Herm. The coastlines of the two largest islands can be walked in a day by the most determined of walkers, but three or four days each allows time to enjoy the scenery and explore some of the features along the way. The smaller islands can be walked around in a day apiece, although two days on Alderney and Sark would allow a much more leisurely appreciation.

So, an average long-distance walker might expect to spend a week and a half walking round the coasts and hopping from island to island, covering up to 178km (110 miles). If the Channel Islands Way is attempted over a two-week holiday there would be plenty of time to enjoy the route without feeling the need to dash from one island to another. The entire coastlines of Guernsey, Alderney, Sark and Herm are covered in this guidebook, while the coastline of Jersey is covered in a companion volume, *Walking on Jersey*. The only other planning materials required would be up-to-date timetables for ferries and flights between the islands, and a schedule aimed at making the best use of time. A basic table of distances is outlined below:

Island	Distance
Jersey	77km (48 miles)
Guernsey	60km (37 miles)
Alderney	19km (11½ miles)
Sark	16km (10 miles)
Herm	6km (4 miles)
Channel Islands Way	178km (110 miles)

APPENDIX B

Route summary table

No	Start	Finish	Distance
	Guernsey		
1	Liberation Monument, St Peter Port	Liberation Monument, St Peter Port	Variable
2	Bus Station, St Peter Port	Bus Station, St Peter Port	6.5km (4 miles)
3	Sausmarez Manor, Fermain	Sausmarez Manor, Fermain	10km (6¼ miles)
4	Bella Luce Hotel, La Fosse	Bella Luce Hotel, La Fosse	10km (6¼ miles)
5	Le Bourg	Le Bourg	11km (7 miles)
6	Les Bruliaux	Les Bruliaux	10km (6¼ miles)
7	Portelet Harbour	Portelet Harbour	5km (3 miles)
8	Portelet Harbour	L'Erée	6.5km (4 miles)
9	La Rocque	La Rocque	11km (7 miles)
10	La Grande Mare Hotel, Vazon Bay	La Grande Mare Hotel, Vazon Bay	9.5km (6 miles)
11	Cobo Kiosk, Cobo	Cobo Kiosk, Cobo	10km (6¼ miles)
12	Port Soif	Port Soif	11km (7 miles)
13	Vale Parish Church	Vale Parish Church	12km (7½ miles)

No	Start	Finish	Distance
14	The Bridge, St Sampson	The Bridge, St Sampson	10km (6¼ miles)
15	Beau Sejour Centre, St Peter Port	Beau Sejour Centre, St Peter Port	9km (5½ miles)
16	St Martin's Parish Church	St Martin's Parish Church	5km (3 miles)
17	St Andrew's Parish Church	St Andrew's Parish Church	7km (4½ miles)
18	King's Mills	King's Mills	9km (5½ miles)
19	Rocquaine Bay	Rocquaine Bay	6km (3¾ miles)
20	Liberation Monument, St Peter Port	Liberation Monument, St Peter Port	63.5km (39 miles)
Alderney			
21	St Anne's Parish Church	St Anne's Parish Church	12km (7½ miles)
22	St Anne's Parish Church	St Anne's Parish Church	12km (7½ miles)
Sark			
23	The Avenue, The Village	The Avenue, The Village	15km (9½ miles)
24	The Avenue, The Village	The Avenue, The Village	10km (6¼ miles)
Herm			
25	The Harbour	The Harbour	6.5km (4 miles)

APPENDIX C
Contacts

Government – Bailiwick of Guernsey
States of Guernsey, www.gov.gg
States of Alderney, www.alderney.gov.gg
Chief Pleas of Sark, www.gov.sark.gg

Tourist information
Guernsey Information Centre, North Plantation, St Peter Port, GY1 2LQ, tel.
01481 723552, email enquiries@visitguernsey.com, website
www.visitguernsey.com
States of Alderney, PO Box 1, Alderney, GY9 3AA, tel. 01481 822811,
www.visitalderney.com
Sark, www.sark.info
Herm, www.herm.com

History and heritage
Guernsey Museum, Candie Gardens, St Peter Port, GY1 1UG, tel. 01481 726518.
Guernsey Museums and Galleries service, www.museum.guernsey.net
La Société Guernesiaise, tel. 01481 725093, www.societe.org.gg
The Alderney Society, Alderney Museum, www.alderneysociety.org
La Société Sercquaise, Visitor Centre, Sark, www.socsercq.sark.gg
National Trust of Guernsey, 26 Cornet Street, St Peter Port, GY1 1LF, tel. 01481
728451, www.nationaltrust-gsy.org.gg
Channel Islands Occupation Society, www.occupied.guernsey.net

Air travel
Flybe, tel. 0871 7002000, www.flybe.com
Aurigny, tel. 01481 822886, www.aurigny.com
Blue Islands, tel. 08456 202122, www.blueislands.com
Channel Islands Travel Service, tel. 01534 496600, www.guernseytravel.com

Ferry travel
Condor, tel. 0845 6091024, www.condorferries.co.uk
Manche Îles Express, tel. 01534 880756, www.manche-iles-express.com
Travel Trident, tel. 01481 721379 (Guernsey) or 01481 722377 (Herm)
Isle of Sark Shipping Co, tel. 01481 724059, www.sarkshippingcompany.com

Bus services
Island Coachways, Guernsey, tel. 01481 720210, www.icw.gg/buses.
There are no bus services on Alderney, Sark or Herm.

Communications
Sure Cable & Wireless, www.surecw.com
Guernsey Post, www.guernseypost.com

Map and map sales
States of Guernsey 1:15,000 Digital Map
Alderney, Sark and Herm 1:10,000 Digital Map
Digimap, Guernsey, tel. 01481 700321, www.digimap.gg
Stanfords, tel. 020 78361321, www.stanfords.co.uk
The Map Shop, tel. 0800 0854080, www.themapshop.co.uk
Cordee, tel. 01455 611185, www.cordee.co.uk

Emergency Contacts
Police, ambulance, fire and coastguard services, tel. 999 or 112.
Channel Islands Air Search, www.ci-airsearch.com

Walking the Channel Islands Way will lead walkers onwards to explore the coast of Jersey too

LISTING OF CICERONE GUIDES

For full information on all our
guides, and to order books
and eBooks, visit our website:
www.cicerone.co.uk.

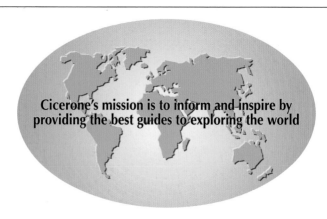

Cicerone's mission is to inform and inspire by providing the best guides to exploring the world

Since its foundation 40 years ago, Cicerone has specialised in publishing guidebooks and has built a reputation for quality and reliability. It now publishes nearly 300 guides to the major destinations for outdoor enthusiasts, including Europe, UK and the rest of the world.

Written by leading and committed specialists, Cicerone guides are recognised as the most authoritative. They are full of information, maps and illustrations so that the user can plan and complete a successful and safe trip or expedition – be it a long face climb, a walk over Lakeland fells, an alpine cycling tour, a Himalayan trek or a ramble in the countryside.

With a thorough introduction to assist planning, clear diagrams, maps and colour photographs to illustrate the terrain and route, and accurate and detailed text, Cicerone guides are designed for ease of use and access to the information.

If the facts on the ground change, or there is any aspect of a guide that you think we can improve, we are always delighted to hear from you.

Cicerone Press
2 Police Square Milnthorpe Cumbria LA7 7PY
Tel: 015395 62069 Fax: 015395 63417
info@cicerone.co.uk www.cicerone.co.uk